MY REGIMENT AND ME

The Coldstream Guards in UK and the Suez Canal Emergencies 1951-1956

Les Walklin

Published by Honeybee Books, Dorset
www.honeybeebooks.co.uk

Printed in the UK using paper from sustainable sources

ISBN: 978-1-910616-65-9

Contents

List of Photographs

Acknowledgements

I wish to thank Lieutenant General Sir James Bucknall KCB CBE, the Colonel of the Regiment, for reading the manuscript and for writing the Foreword. I am grateful for his support and encouragement and it is heartening to know that high ranking officers such as he truly values each and every one of their Guardsmen and old Coldstreamers too. I am much in his debt.

Thanks are also due to Major Sir Edward Crofton, a true Coldstreamer, for his very considerable help in facilitating the publication and managing Regimental protocol thereby assuring a positive outcome.

Thanks to Maggie Snook, the Dorset and West Hants Canal Zoners Organiser for persuading me to write this book fearing that like many other veterans' stories mine too would die with me. So I have put on record what I recall of service life with particular reference to postings to Cyprus and Egypt.

Although the content contains a commentary on soldiering with the Regiment, I have sought to capture the experiences and kind of training experienced by the thousands of recruits joining HM Forces in the 1950s. The living and working conditions of the many thousands of servicemen and women who served in the Canal Zone during the Suez Emergencies is outlined and readers will perhaps appreciate the somewhat dangerous and miserable times endured by what has been termed 'the forgotten army'.

I am indebted to Patricia Jezzard, President of the Canal Zoners for contributing the final chapter entitled '60 Years On', the result of her substantial researches into the Suez Crisis of 1956. Patricia works tirelessly to manage the 2 000 strong association of surviving Suez veterans and the members are fortunate to have such a tower of strength at the helm.

I would like to pay tribute to the memory of the late Colonel R J V Crichton CVO MC our revered Commanding Officer of the 1st Battalion with whom I served in Egypt, for excerpts from his book, '*The Coldstream Guards 1946-1970*'.

Lastly, I am grateful to Chella and Sophie at Honeybee Books for their unstinting support in producing this book.

ACKNOWLEDGEMENTS

I wish to thank Lieutenant General Sir James Bucknall KCB CBE, the Colonel of the Regiment, for reading the manuscript and for writing the Foreword. I am grateful for his support and encouragement, and it is heartening to know that such senior officers such as he truly values each and every one of their [illegible] and the consequences too. I am much in his debt.

Thanks are also due to Major Sir Edward Crofton, a true Coldstreamer, for his very considerable help in facilitating the publication and [illegible] of the [illegible] assuring a positive outcome.

[illegible] and [illegible] for [illegible] me to write this book [illegible] with me [illegible] to [illegible].

[illegible]

the [illegible].

I am [illegible] President of the [illegible] for [illegible] 1956 [illegible].

I would like to [illegible] the late [illegible] Commanding Officer of [illegible] for [illegible] excerpts from his book [illegible].

Lastly I am grateful to Charles and [illegible] Books for their [illegible] in producing this book.

FOREWORD

By
Lieutenant General Sir James Bucknall, KCB CBE
29th Colonel of the Regiment

All too often people go through life without making a formal record of their experiences, challenges and achievements. I am delighted that Mr Walklin has been persuaded to put on record something of his time in the Regiment.

He has given a fascinating account of his Regimental service, containing many humorous incidents which have been incorporated into a living snapshot of life in the military at that time. His recollection of his training at the Guards Depot leads one to reflect that the regime then was arguably more Spartan than that which currently exists! His active service in Cyprus and Egypt with the 1st Battalion during the Suez Canal Emergency, and his subsequent recall from the Reserves for the Suez Crisis in 1956, highlight events that have been important episodes in the annals of Coldstream Regimental History.

Throughout his service, his loyalty and dedication have epitomised the ethos and traditions of our great Regiment. He has indeed been part of 'a same company of men whom God made the instruments of great things', and who have lived up to our motto, Second to None.

I recommend this book to all Coldstreamers, both past and present.

James Bucknall

About Myself

I enlisted in the Coldstream Guards on 27th November 1950. After recruit training at the Guards Depot I joined the 1st Battalion in June 1951 and served with that Battalion until my discharge from the Army in November 1955. On 9th August 1956 I was recalled to the Colours and the 3rd Battalion as Transport Sergeant for the Suez Crisis, for a period of 118 days.

I hold the Regiment in the highest esteem, always did and always will. For me the Regiment is my family and I value beyond measure the gentlemen and other ranks with whom I served. Its discipline, effectiveness, efficiency and comradeship shaped my life, and I am eternally grateful for the 'I can do this' attitude that it bred in me. I believe that I have never let the Regiment down and shall always love it.

Introduction

Hard times - Les Walklin's early life

All too often people go through life without making a formal record of their experiences, challenges and achievements but the Canal Zoner's Association's Dorset Local Organiser persuaded the author to put on record something of his time with the garrison in Egypt.

He would lead an unplanned and fate driven life that propels him from extreme poverty as a boy to being quite well-off with recognition as an educational writer, engineering lecturer and training consultant.

His father was born and bred into country ways, labouring and working with horses hauling coal and later a brewer's dray. Driving teams of horses prompted him to volunteer to join the Royal Engineers where he was employed as a driver of horse-drawn wagons conveying ammunition and rations to front line units. He served throughout the First World War from 1914 to 1919. He was fortunate to survive, as he had suffered serious shrapnel wounds at Salonika and during the Gallipoli Campaign. He didn't say much about the war but his son did notice a horrendous scar on his stomach when helping him get dressed. It was then that he told how awful it was lying there helpless surrounded by dead and dying troops.

Les was only 10 when his father was run over by a railway engine losing his right arm and leg. Sadly, he died a year later leaving his wife destitute with little money to bring up his two children. They were extremely hard up having received only £350 compensation, doled out at £2 per week for three years. Losing that income made them really poor. Unable to afford gaslight the family sat in candlelight with mother hardly touching her share of the rations. She went without in order to sustain her children.

Although winning a Scholarship for Reading School Les didn't enrol there - couldn't afford the fees, sports gear and books. Poverty forced him to leave school aged 14 and work as a trainee truck mechanic. His wages were 14/- (70 pence) for a 44-hour week.

Aged 15 his mother was institutionalised - the grinding poverty and money worries had taken its toll on her and she had a nervous breakdown. This left Les in a distressed state but fortunately for him a neighbour who'd worked with his mum at Huntley & Palmers Biscuit Factory during WW1 packing hard-tack biscuits for the army took him in.

He decides to join the Coldstream Guards. Raised by General Monck in 1650 it is the oldest English regiment with continuous service in the British Army. In writing this book Les hopes to proudly endorse its motto 'Nulli Secundus' - 'Second to None.'

Les tells in words and pictures his story that is partly autobiographical and partly historical. It covers the 1st and 3rd Battalions of the Coldstream Guards postings on 'active service' to Cyprus and Egypt during the Suez Canal Zone Emergency from 1951 - 1954 and the 1956 Suez Crisis preparations.

The content combines humorous incidents from a soldier's viewpoint told using some soldier's expressions and NCO's expletive vocabulary merged with a kind of living history of the time. A few references to 'pop' social psychology with applications to boredom and obedience are included, together with descriptions of the Celebration of Ramadan, the Cyprus Troubles, the Defence of Hougoumont Farm at Waterloo and the symbolic custom of 'Hanging the Brick' at Xmas.

The book gives an account with many amusing anecdotes of a young man from a poverty stricken background who joins the Coldstream Guards in 1950 and progresses through the military training at the fearsome Guards Depot where he endures 16 weeks of harsh parade drill and physical training. This is followed by 12 weeks of weapon training and fieldcraft before passing out as a fully trained guardsman after the final Battle Training on the Yorkshire Moors.

He is posted to the 1st Battalion based in Windsor where he undertakes guard duties and joins the Mechanical Transport (MT) Platoon. This proves to be a route to rapid promotion and a fulfilling role for his entire service with the Regiment.

Before long due to rioting and terrorist activity the Battalion is hurriedly shipped out to Cyprus aboard the aircraft carrier HMS *Illustrious* and shortly afterwards to the Suez Canal Zone. Then follows an account of the various deployments and duties undertaken between 1951 and 1953 until departing for UK aboard a troopship bound for Liverpool.

While the story told provides a true historical account of the Regiment's life and times in Cyprus and Egypt it also contains sometimes amusing commentary on living in basic camps, enduring periods of boredom, unpleasant circumstances and activities such as guard duties, driving in the desert, searching villages and safeguarding personal and military kit from the ever present 'klefti wallahs'.

Les describes not only the vehicle types and duties undertaken but also recounts quite amusing stories about the incoming Transport Officer; a very posh gentleman who was to become his lifelong friend. Quite unsuited to the role he didn't appear to know the difference between the bonnet and back axle of a truck.

The return of the 1st Battalion to UK is followed by its various activities, including the Bank of England Piquet, Windsor Castle Guard and Training Reservists. Les tells an amusing story of Major Richard Carr-Gomm's antics at Company Orders and comments on his later selfless life as the 'Scrubbing Major' after Les and he leave the Regiment.

On a more serious tone the activities of murderous terrorists are outlined. These include ambushes, sniping and attacks on civilians including the murder of a Nun, riots at the Tel-el-Kebir Railway Station and fire-fights with well armed Egyptian Police at the Bureau de Sanitaire in Ismailia. The 3rd Battalion is flown to Fayid from Tripoli as part of a task force of 20 000 reinforcements and based at Tel-el-Kebir before moving to Fanara where it remained until returning to UK.

Then due to the 1956 Suez Crisis, Les a Class 'A' Reservist, is recalled from Civvy Street as the 3rd Battalion Transport Sergeant. He describes the mobilisation and the subsequent 'It's on' - false alarm -'No, it's off' indecision and preparations to join the fray.

Les pays tribute to absent friends and those who didn't return and to the Canal Zoners brotherhood before reflecting on the handling of the Suez Crisis.

The final chapter containing a carefully researched and recorded account of the '1956 Suez Crisis 60 Years Ago' provided by Patricia Jezzard, President of the 2 000 strong 'The Canal Zoners' association' gives a factual picture of the whole unfortunate incident.

1
The Guards Depot at Caterham

In the beginning

Impulsively when aged 18 the author joined the Coldstream Guards. Keen to 'make a man of himself' he visited the Recruiting Office in Reading where the Recruiting Sergeant interviewed him. On hearing his wish to enlist in the Coldstream Guards the Recruiter rubbed his hands with apparent joy. A civilian doctor gave Les a quick medical and was found to be *alive, warm and breathing*. Then followed a few verbal questions testing his language skills by reading and writing simple phrases. He passed but perhaps he should have known better than to sign on the dotted line as a regular. However, being enticed by the lure of enhanced pay rather than getting the measly 28 shillings a week that conscripted National Servicemen received, he had signed on. Had he known what he was to endure he might have changed his mind.

At the Guards Depot

Having enlisted on 27 November 1950 and received my King's Shilling I was issued with a railway warrant and bus fares and ordered to report to the Guards Depot, Caterham. The bus conductor smiled in a knowing way when I asked him to set me down there. I soon found out why. There was a lunatic asylum situated next door!

I ambled through the iron gates and entered the guardroom. There was a sergeant seated behind a desk and I rather stupidly blurted out, 'I've come to join the army.'

'Orderly!' bawled the sergeant to a cringing recruit standing nearby, presumably on some kind of fatigue duty there.

'Yes sergeant,' he croaked.

'Take him to the Receiving Room.'

We set of at rocket speed with my guide babbling on about people collapsing, driven crazy and dropping dead as we hurried past the square and soon reached the building. It had been a stable block with high walls and a few small windows close to the ceiling. There I found a few newcomers lounging on striped mattresses on top of old cast iron bedsteads with springs stretched over frames. The fellows didn't look too happy and I felt a sinking feeling in my stomach. What had I let myself in for!

Before long an NCO appeared who marched us to the stores where we 'drew-up' three damp blankets, a hard cylindrical palliase and a pillowcase that we were instructed to stuff with straw. That comprised our bedding. Then back to the Receiving Room where we dumped the kit. The NCO then directed us to the NAAFI where we could buy a drink and something to eat before returning to the stable to make up our beds and get some sleep.

I recall steam rising from the blankets the following morning as the dampness evaporated. We were awakened by the sound of marching men. Hob nailed boots hammering down on the tarmac road outside. 'Left right leeeft!' screamed a PT Instructor driving them onward.

Climbing up onto the iron bed heads and looking through the windows we could just see what was going on. It was a squad of shaven-headed barelegged recruits wearing greatcoats and ammo boots with their socks rolled down. Each man carried a white towel under his left arm en-route to the gym at an unearthly hour. It was bitterly cold and I was horrified seeing the captive victims for the first time. Thinking it's too late to worry now I sat down with my head in my hands wondering just what had possessed me to sign on.

For starters we'd been issued with a one-pint china mug, knife, fork and spoon, shirt and underclothes, ammo boots, a few other necessities and dressed in a set of denims and dark blue beret (now khaki coloured) and this is what we managed with until full kit was issued. Our civilian clothes were packed into boxes and posted to our home address, as we'd have no need for these for the foreseeable future.

Our Trained Soldier

Before long we were moved into a long barrack room where we were left in the care of an experienced older guardsman with the appointment of 'Trained Soldier'.

'Right,' says he gathering us together, 'you'll find Regimental life here vastly different from what you've been used to. But you'll need to adjust quickly to the discipline and life now you're in the Brigade of Guards.' He went on, 'You'll need to learn to obey orders without question. That's discipline. You'll learn what integrity and loyalty to the Regiment and to your mates means. And you'll learn what respect for others means. Then whatever situation you find yourselves in you'll know what to do. That is, you'll instinctively do the right thing.'

'Boy, what an inspirational greeting that was.' I said to a mate.

'What's the daily routine Trained Soldier?' someone asked.

'I'll get round to telling you all about it bit by bit. But basically you'll get out of bed, wash, have breakfast, clean the barrack room, dress for drill or PT, go and do it, have dinner, afternoon parades and finish up with your evening meal.'

'Then it's a two-hour kit maintenance shining parade and kit inspection. If all goes well you'll get a bit of relaxation before 'question time' and 'hands and feet inspection' and lights out. If it doesn't go well you'll face the consequences. All your kit will thrown out of the window.'

'Trained Soldier, what's question time?' blurted out a Londoner.

'When your Superintending Sergeant comes to inspect you and your kit in the evening he'll question you on Regimental history and Battle Honours. You'll have to learn them all. But particularly everything about the one painted on the wall above your own bed. See all those painted above every bed? And tell him about the flags too. But you'll get time to learn them.'

My first question came from the Superintending Sergeant a week later. 'Tell me about your battle honour, *Inkerman*. Don't say, "I think." I want the facts. You're not paid to think. You're paid to know and do as you're told.'

'We suffered heavily, Sergeant. The Coldstream Regiment lost 8 officers killed and 5 wounded, with 181 guardsmen as casualties. The Russians fought bravely but we fought harder and won the day. Our Victorian forerunners just wouldn't give way. The battle must have been ferocious 'cos 12 Victoria Crosses were awarded to British soldiers for actions in the battle.'

'That's a good answer but I'll want more detail next time.'

Our Trained Soldier was a kind of father figure to us, but one who'd not tolerate poor standards or idleness in any shape or form. We thought a lot of him. This was a man who was skilled in all aspects of soldiering and especially cleaning kit, assembling various orders of dress and acceptable turnout. And he had obviously seen action during the Second World War too, although he never mentioned it.

'The cleanliness of the barrack room will be maintained by sweeping, dusting and a daily liberal application of this orange coloured wax polish to the woodwork. You'll then buff the floor to perfection by heaving heavy bumpers to and fro over the wooden planks. You'll expend a lot of elbow grease. After you've done you'll move across the dark shiny surface treading on cloths. No footprints or dust will be allowed.'

'Thanks for that Trained Soldier,' someone grumbled.

Medical matters

Within a few days we were off to the Medical Centre for a medical and a system of grading physical and mental fitness known as the PULHHEEMS classification. It's an abbreviation for the testing: Physique, Upper limbs, Lower limbs including the back, Hearing (left), Hearing (right), Eyesight left, Eyesight right, Mental function and emotional Stability. The latter two provided an opportunity for those National Servicemen wishing to escape the rigours of training to 'work their ticket'.

Having completed these checks the Medical Officer moved on to examine the recruits' sexual health.

'Listen up all of you. Sexual health is an important part of a soldier's overall physical and emotional well-being. Avoidance of sexually transmitted diseases is critically important and we'll look into that shortly. But during the Free From Infection (FFI) inspection I shall be asking you individually whether or not you suffer from a medical condition known as erectile dysfunction.'

'What's that?' piped up one of the recruits.

'Quite simply it means that you can't get IT up. When you're sexually stimulated you can't get your cock hard enough to penetrate your partner. Some medical practitioners call it impotence. If you suffer from this it can affect your emotional stability and your performance in action. But don't accuse us of controlling your libido by putting bromide in the tea!'

Another comedian interrupted, 'Well it won't make a lot of difference to us in here. We're not allowed out.'

Ignoring the intervention the doctor went on, 'Fortunately there is a range of treatments available to improve matters. So don't be ashamed to discuss your problem with me or later with your unit Medical Officer. Right, now get in line for the FFI.'

The medical officer commenced the FFI inspection otherwise known as a 'short arm inspection'. It's a check for signs of Venereal Disease (VD) and infestation by 'crabs on the rocks' or other nasties. For new recruits it was a bit embarrassing the first time a white-coated Medical Officer asked you to drop your trousers and stand there with your underpants around your ankles; while he, reeking of disinfectant, asked a number of questions.

'Do you feel any pain when you're urinating?'

'No, Sir.'

'Do you have penile discharge?'

'What's that?' asked the bloke in front of me.

'Green or yellow puss leaking from your cock!'

'No, sir.'

'Right. Bend over and touch your toes.'

Having checked the recruit's buttocks for signs of Herpes he proceeded to scan his 'privates' looking for signs of bacterial infection, swollen testicles, blisters, scabs and 'blobby knobs'.

This was followed by an eyesight colour-blindness test. Then we joined a queue for TAB inoculations injected by means of a very blunt needle that resulted in painful swollen arms. Finally we made a 'voluntary donation' of a pint of blood after which the donor was rewarded with a mug of sweet tea.

Later in order to strike the fear of goodness into us a series of films designed to put one off sexual encounters supplemented the medical. Shots of unfortunates who'd not been too fussy about where they stuck their knobs were featured with close-ups of advanced gonorrhoea and incurable final stage tertiary syphilis sufferers. Men with unmistakable signs of sexually transmitted diseases such as blistered rotting flesh, brain damage, heart problems, uncontrollable nervous diseases and lunatic behaviour. It served its purpose for most and was further reinforced by stories told of patients screaming as white-coated medical practitioners rammed red-hot metal needles into the infected urethra to burn off inflamed tissue.

It was enough to permanently put one off casual sexual encounters and the subsequent lure of foreign prostitutes. But later it was rumoured that the legendary Madam Peg Leg, a one-legged French 'sex worker', was kept busy in Egypt until terrorists summarily executed her for fraternising with the hated Infidels. Her 'jig-a-jig Johnnie' pimp's hoard of piastres being 'confiscated' before he too met with the same fate.

Once posted to a battalion should a guardsman report sick hoping to be 'excused duty' but be considered fit enough for duty he would be classified either as 'fit for duty' or 'malingering'. The best he could hope for would be M&D, that is, Medicine and Duty and think himself lucky enough to avoid being put on a charge. But because malingering is intentionally fabricating or exaggerating the symptoms of mental or physical disorders the malingerer would pay a heavy price if caught out.

Medicine on offer comprised either Gentian Violet Lotion that has antibacterial properties or the No.9 pill (the pill that cured all ills). These two items were the Medical Officer's commonly prescribed medication. Gentian Violet was applied externally to treat infections such as athlete's foot, jock itch, ringworm and impetigo because antibiotics weren't available. It tended to remedy or soothe such infections. The No.9 pill covered just about every other ailment.

Life before squadding

Recruits were marched to the Barber's Shop where the barber armed with an electric shaver stood amidst piles of hair ready to give them a 'short back and sides' or 'over the top' shearing.

'Don't want you to end up lousy do we,' he said as he sheared each one, 'your mates won't want blood-sucking lice crawling all over them will they?'

Then light-headed they reported to the Quartermaster Stores and were issued with a full compliment of kit including ill-fitting uniforms, off-white webbing, knobbly boots and green brasses. This would keep them busy during the daily two-hour evening shining parades during which absolute silence and no smoking was enforced. It involved vigorously applying Blanco to webbing, polishing brasses with Bluebell metal polish and intensive spit and polishing boots with Kiwi Black Parade polish.

They'd have to carry out daily fatigues and wait until enough regular recruits appeared before they could commence training. They were trapped, imprisoned and cocooned from society.

Whilst on fatigues one day an older soldier gave us some good advice. He explained how an old army adage could keep soldiers out of trouble. He said, 'Keep busy and always remember this. "If it moves, salute it. If it doesn't move, pick it up. If you can't pick it up, paint it". Or get a clipboard and walk about smartly with it displayed in an obvious position. Bullshit baffles brains.'

Before long I was to put his advice into practice but make an awfully embarrassing mistake.

Soon afterwards while on fatigues sweeping the area in front of Monck Block I put part one part of the adage into action. As I pushed my broom I noticed a majestically attired figure approaching. The person could be clearly seen marching briskly toward me. He was wearing a forage cap with a white band around it. Brilliantly shining sword hanging from a white belt. Wooden stick under his arm. 'Mmm, could be an officer. Better throw him one up when he gets nearer.' Getting closer! 'Hmm.' I was now convinced that it was an officer so I sprang to attention and stood transfixed with my broom clutched upright against my left thigh. I was ready to salute him as he passed by and gave what I thought to be a smart salute. The man strode across to me. Seeing that I obviously didn't have a clue about such things he said, 'No lad. I'm a Warrant Officer. You only salute officers' and with that he smartly turned about and disappeared from view. I felt a really stupid twat and never forgot the incident. I learned later that the man was WO2 (Drill Sgt) Dougie Glisson a man to be respected and feared when as RSM of the 3rd Battalion I was to meet him on my recall for the 1956 Suez Crisis.

Whitewashing static objects was a frequent fatigue task. Carefully applying thick white liquid with a floppy brush to all the short posts marking the boundaries of the square and grassy areas was a must. 'Don't drop any on the tarmac or you'll have to lick it up.' It was even rumoured that over-zealous recruits wanting to win barrack room competitions had removed upper layers of coal from the black bunker painted white inside, then washed the coal before whitewashing it and replacing it.

I didn't try the clipboard ruse as I feared getting caught and was too insignificant to rise to the occasion. In fact I felt so small that I could crawl under a snake's belly while wearing a top hat. But I felt that it was all part of a proven psychological approach designed to cleanse recruits of all undesirable traits and reward good deeds, thereby building them up as decent responsible soldiers.

For some reason we regulars appeared to be segregated from the National Service conscripts who'd opted to join the Regiment or who'd been coerced to swell the ranks. For some it was the choice of either enlisting or working down the coalmines.

I won't rabbit on about the first few weeks but eventually there were enough regular recruits to form a squad and at long last training could begin.

We were to learn the hard way that here in the Guards Depot the emphasis would be on drill and harsh discipline. This was the place where the words of Hebrews 12:11 would be applied: *'No discipline seems pleasant at the time, but painful. Later on however, it produces a harvest of righteousness and peace for those who have been trained by it.'* In our case it produced fearless highly disciplined guardsmen!

But today the changes in the procedures for maintaining discipline have meant that all those in authority have to adopt a vastly different approach to the methods employed and the conduct of characters I encountered as a recruit!

2

The Barracks

What a fearsome place the Guards Depot Caterham was! Completed in 1877, initially there were four two-storey barrack blocks supplemented by Officers', Sergeants' and Trained Soldiers' Messes, Quartermaster Stores, a cookhouse, a laundry, coal yard, workshops, stables and hospital. A Guardroom with detention cells near the entrance completed the Depot buildings. Provision was made for a large barrack square with three Drill Sheds constructed so that training could go on even during inclement weather. Two more blocks were subsequently added and later converted to three storeys. The Guards Chapel was erected there in 1885.

Monck Block was named after General Monck, 1st Duke of Albemarle who commanded Monck's Regiment of Foot, originally formed by Cromwell in 1650. The Regiment was incorporated in Charles II's standing army where it became known as the Coldstream Guards. It therefore became the home of Coldstreamers stationed there. Quite apart from raving instructors making one's life a misery 24/7, it was a bleak, ancient brick and stone building with cold draughty barrack rooms in which we were housed. A thoroughly inhospitable place to live or should I say exist.

Hygiene

There were no showers in the washrooms but we recruits were frequently quick-marched to a nearby shower block where due to winter coal shortages there was no hot water. There we shivered as we bathed in icy water under the watchful eye of a sadistic corporal who recorded our names in a book, having satisfied himself that we'd actually showered rather than just wetted our hair. The washrooms allocated to each barrack room had long granite sinks with only cold water drawn from highly polished brass taps. That's where we completed our 'ablutions' i.e. washed and shaved in order to *'maintain health and prevent the spreading of diseases'*. Although the facility was really basic we made the most of it fearing that unless we kept ourselves spotlessly clean we'd suffer a fate worse than death. Each evening before 'lights-out' the Superintending Sergeant would enter the barrack room screaming, 'On your beds. Hands and feet inspection.' We'd then have to lift each foot in turn and avoid wobbling about which would incur his wrath. He would then cast his eagle eyes on our outstretched arms and finger nails to check for 'filth'. Should anyone be found lacking they'd be frog-marched to the washroom and 'scrubbed' with cold water, bristle broom and scrubbing brush. A very unpleasant punishment.

Hygiene included regular 'blanket shaking'. We were frequently made to strip our beds and carry our blankets downstairs to a space in the fresh air where we were ordered to 'vigorously shake the blankets'. This was intended to cast out any uninvited bedbugs or fleas that had found their way into our blankets.

We were told that bedbugs hide under or within the mattress or close to where you sleep and because their bodies are flat they can squeeze into the smallest space. Favoured hideouts included a mattress seam where females lay their eggs or the joints of the bed frame. This can make them very difficult to spot. Our remedy was to use our lighters as mini flame-throwers steering the tip of the flame along the mattress seams. Alternatively a lighted candle was used when available. If only we had the powerful suction of a cordless Dyson V6 cleaner to get the little sods.

Their eggs hatch after about 10 days and shed their skin leaving mottled brown shells on the mattress. Attracted by your body heat, the bugs crawl out at night to bite your exposed skin and feed on your blood, just as mosquitoes do.

The supervising NCO usually issued a warning: 'Don't forget to look out for black spots on your mattress where they've shit on it. And check your sheets for blood spots where you may have rolled over and squashed a bug after it'd fed! Keep your mattress free of the little fuckers. If your mattress gets heavily infested it'll be burned and you'll have to pay 'barrack room damages' for a replacement!'

Mess room procedures

I managed to put on a bit of weight and this was undoubtedly due to the sufficient and wholesome cookhouse meals. Unlike the civilians who were still being rationed in the 1950s we had more than enough of 'all-in' stew and filling meals. Our weekly rations per person included about

5lbs of meat, 8oz of bacon, nearly a pound of butter or margarine, 4oz of cheese, 8oz of jam, 2lbs of sugar and 4oz of tea.

Mealtimes in the communal Guardsman's Mess Room were supervised by a Duty L/Cpl who strolled about making sure no breaches of defined routine occurred. Each man armed with his own knife, fork and spoon would pick up two china plates. Then he would join an orderly queue slowly shuffling toward the counter where a row of cooks would ladle the various foodstuffs onto his plate. The same applied to the pudding. 'No pushing or shoving. Just wait for your turn.'

Whilst the meal was being consumed an officer followed by the senior cook and the Duty L/Cpl clutching a clipboard and pen patrolled the tables.

'Any complaints or suggestions?' enquired the officer.

Not a word of response would be heard. Far to dangerous to complain. For to do so would undoubtedly result in the complainant's name being taken by the L/Cpl and his comment recorded. The outcome would be additional cookhouse or mess room fatigues that would *'enable him to implement his improvement or suggestion'*.

But one could ask the officer for permission to go to the servery for 'seconds'.

A strictly enforced rule was that tea must be poured into each mug in turn. *'No dipping your mug into the bucket!'* But on one occasion Recruit Larry Milne, one of my squad mates, got up from his seat at the table and hurried around it to where the stainless steel tea bucket was being passed from one to another in the prescribed manner. But Larry couldn't wait for the bucket to get to him and dipped his china mug into the bucket. The watchful L/Cpl saw him do this and hurled a carving knife across the room hitting Larry's hand causing it to bleed profusely. So it was off to the Medical Inspection Room for Larry. Later when questioned about the incident Larry lied, 'I accidentally cut it with my knife, Sir.'

To incriminate an NCO by reporting unfair or harsh treatment of any kind was unforgivable. To complain about anything was definitely a 'No No'. Some thought about contacting a newspaper or an officer but the thought of every NCO closing ranks and making one's life an ongoing misery was an effective deterrent. In any case the rule was *'obey the order and complain afterwards.'* But nobody ever reported anything as far as I know.

From the start we obeyed the unwritten law of *'never complain to anyone about anything'* but if we really needed to we could relate our grievance to a Regimental SNCO or officer. Worse still never complain anonymously. This is the concept handed down since the Duke of Wellington during the Peninsula Wars said, *'To write an anonymous letter is the meanest action of which any man can be guilty.'*

Physical training

As fast as we added weight the Physical Training Instructors (PTIs) ensured that we lost it and transformed our daily intake into useful muscle. Our PTI's behaved like psychopaths. *'Training's tough. Our job is to get you into shape, build up your stamina and strength and that's what we're gonna do!'*

Physically at the peak of condition they were masters of all they surveyed both within the gymnasium and in the open too. I didn't like the physical training sessions. For me it was absolute torture. Designed to build up muscle, stamina and to mentally challenge the recruit it was extremely demanding. Before signing on, even while at school, I'd avoided exercise whenever I could. Rather than walking I'd catch a bus, ride where I needed to go on a pushbike and later on mount my trusty BSA 250 cc motorbike.

Before enlisting I'd got enough exercise at work as a heavy goods truck mechanic and I have this to thank for building up strong muscular forearms and shoulders. Striving to change a back road spring and cursing while unscrewing the rusted huge 'U bolt' nuts securing the spring to the axle or undoing large wheel nuts took a bit of doing. But it came in useful later during muscle strengthening exercises involving grabbing the .303 Lee Enfield at its barrel end and raising and lowering the rifle with outstretched arms. Sheer torture. Weakness was rewarded with, *'Run around the hut with your rifle above your head until I tell you to stop. That'll strengthen your arms.'*

Thinking back to the physical training sessions I recall the PTI screaming in a high-pitched voice, 'On the wall bars - UP.' This meant that we needed to rush across the gym, jump up onto the nearest set of equispaced wooden bars and climb up until we reached the ceiling. Last man up received an unpleasant punishment. Then followed a short warm-up by jogging on the spot and prescribed exercises: stretching while lying prone, deep breathing, horse work, forward rolls, lunges, squats, press-ups, pull-ups, scrambling up the wall bars, rope climbing, bear crawls on all fours and any other painful exercise he could think of before the final cool down. Not being a 'keep-fit' fan I couldn't wait for the ordeal to end.

Thankfully the physical exercises strengthened most muscles and especially the leg muscles, which enabled me to complete the compulsory basic training two-mile run and forced marches within the time allowed.

We were required to participate in a three two-minute rounds boxing session. Size and weight was not considered. No gum shields, protective helmets or lightweight gloves just PT kit and heavy leather gloves.

'You and you get in there and knock the shit out of one another. If you don't put your utmost into it, I'll get in there with you', crowed the super fit PTI.

'Deck him, deck him!' roared the fired-up onlookers who'd obviously enjoyed their Saturday night pub fights and brawling in civvy street.

'If you can't hack it there's worse things in store for you, so get in there!' goaded the PTI.

Weakling Walklin didn't enjoy that activity but it had to be endured.

Church parade

The Guards' Sgt-in-Waiting role known as Orderly Sgt in some units is a weeklong duty by SNCOs who receive daily instructions from the RSM.

If a recruit felt the need to pray for deliverance from the ongoing ordeal or was a true Believer he could give his name to the Sgt-in-Waiting and be placed on the nominal roll for the regular Sunday morning service held in the Depot's Guards Chapel. This would mean that he would need to 'fall in' and be inspected wearing his Service Dress Cap with polished chin strap and regimental cap star, khaki shirt with woollen tie, best battledress, web belt, boots and anklets. This placed him in a vulnerable position with a high probability of being 'stopped' for alleged dirty belt or chinstrap brasses, Blanco quality inadequate, crooked tie or polished boots not up to required standard. This would lead to a number of *'show cleans'* to be inspected on one or more late night 'defaulters' parades. Alternatively there was a considerable risk of being put on an *'idle on parade'* charge, which would subsequently result in being *'marched in'* on Company Orders where the Company Commander would award several *'extra drills'*. These high speed drills were completed during *'punishment parades'* when the Sgt-in-Waiting would *'chase'* the defaulters wearing FSMO around the barrack square ordering foot drills in (very) quick time and various rifle exercises on the march. Either of these parades could easily result in further show cleans or idle on parade charges. No, it just wasn't worth the risk for an hour or so of peace in the chapel. Better to ignore the verses from Exodus: *'Six days you shall labour and do all your work, but the seventh day you shall not do any work.'* Much safer to attend the inevitable alternative fatigue parades and in private pray for forgiveness.

Fatigues

Coal fatigue

Coal fatigue was a regular Sunday morning task for some poor unfortunates. Forget the seventh day shall be a day of rest. Prepare yourself for a morning's toil. Two of you humping a large galvanised bathtub filled with the weekly coal ration up slippery iron steps to married quarters and elsewhere.

On one such icy cold Sunday morning we recruits paraded awaiting our name to be called by the Sgt-in-Waiting. Each one wondering which task they'd been listed on a roster to perform. Each one hoping that it would be cookhouse fatigue or somewhere warm with the chance of a mug of tea. My name was called and I sprang to attention and marched quickly toward the sergeant. Mistake, idiot I should've been more careful when I pulled my feet in to attention, one-two bang. Sadly my second-best hob-nailed boots skidded on the ice and I fell flat on my back. I got up and was stupid enough to laugh at my mishap.

'Wipe that fucking grin off your face. You're on coal fatigue now. Report to my bunk at 2000 hours. I'll teach you not to laugh on parade.'

With that my companion and me hurried to the coal yard that was stacked with fuel and humped and struggled to deliver to all listed. Hours later on completion it was a cold water wash and a dash to the mess room for Sunday lunch after which I crashed out on my pit for a couple of hours before the evening meal.

I duly reported to the Sgt-in-Waiting five minutes before the appointed time, as was the Regimental custom.

'Right, Walklin, go to Codrington Block and clean the urinals in the piss-house. Stay there until I inspect your work and dismiss you.'

'Yes sergeant', I mumbled and scuttled out of the bunk before he could think of anything to make things worse.

I spent the whole night scraping and scouring the disgusting yellow encrustations from the ancient urinals. But no sign of the sergeant until early next morning as he passed by on his way to make early calls booked by occupants of Codrington Block and rouse the cooks.

'Right, you can fuck off now and think yourself lucky I didn't put you on a charge of disorderly behaviour on parade.'

It was only later that I discovered that Codrington Block was named after Lieutenant General Sir WJ Codrington who'd served with the Coldstream Guards in the 19th. Century and that Major SFB Codrington was currently Officer Commanding No. 3 Company of the 1st Battalion when I joined the Regiment at the Guards Depot. So it appears that the Codrington family was still serving the Regiment well!

Sgt's Mess fatigue

This fatigue normally comprised assisting with the cleansing of vegetables i.e. washing the dirt off root vegetables, washing greens and peeling potatoes before the Cookhouse Sgt could prepare the meals. Then while he and his staff were getting on with the cooking we'd have to wash the dirty breakfast crockery and cutlery, scrub the tables and chairs, mop the floors and dispose of rubbish. We were supplied with hot water for these inside jobs so as it was winter we kept warm.

We didn't have any Army Catering Corps staff. The Regimental Sgt Cook in charge of the cookhouse was a mean and horrible bloke, unpleasant to look at and unkind in his manner. We disliked him intensely due to his harsh treatment of fatigue men working outside in the very cold weather. Outside in freezing temperatures in order to get at the tubers we had to break the ice on large cast iron cauldrons that covered the machine-peeled potatoes left in the open to soak overnight. We then needed to use pointed potato peelers to remove the blackened eyes from the spuds.

'Sgt could we please have some hot water to stop our hands freezing? Our fingers are completely numb getting at the potatoes.'

'This ain't no holiday camp. Fuck off and don't ask again.'

Not even a mug of hot tea. Oh! How we hated him.

Mess room and main cookhouse fatigue

The other-ranks cookhouse fatigue was mainly centred on mopping floors, washing up and scrubbing greasy pots, pans and a mass of crockery and cutlery, although some recruits used their issued knife, fork and spoon. They rinsed their own mug and 'eating irons' in a container filled with lukewarm water that got progressively more greasy and horrible.

The mess-room fatigue involved clearing any rubbish from tabletops and chairs and washing them with disinfectant. Chairs were then arranged in a 'neat and orderly manner'. The floor was then swept and thoroughly mopped again with a powerful disinfectant that later put one off smoking for a while. Rubbish was disposed of according to Standing Orders.

The Duty Mess Room NCO supervised the entire operation, so it had to be completed to perfection or else idlers would be identified, admonished and punished accordingly.

Interior economy

'Stand by your beds.' ordered our Superintending Sergeant on entering the barrack room early on a morning free of parades. 'I'm not satisfied with the state of your bed areas. There's dust and fluff everywhere. Some of you have got bum fluff on your faces and need to shave. The barrack room furniture is filthy. Not a trace of polish on it. Can't see through the windowpanes. Dust on the sills. You've pissed all over the floor in the urinals. The sinks in the washroom are filthy. The taps don't shine. The landing and stairs need sweeping and mopping and the Company area outside is littered. So you'd better get a move on and get it sorted.'

'Trained Soldier, give each man a swabbing task and get them started NOW! Satan might rule the Earth but I rule you lot. Never forget that I can't stand filth. Be assured, a fate worse than death awaits you if I return this evening and find anything not to the required standard.' threatened the Superintending Sergeant.

Truthfully most of his complaints were either figments of his imagination or deliberate wind-ups intended to shake us up. Our Trained Soldier would never have allowed us to leave things imperfectly cleaned and polished.

But nevertheless tasks were allocated and checked on completion.

Then we could rest for an hour or so before hands and feet inspection at 2130 hours. Meanwhile we nervously awaited our fate when the Sergeant carried out his inspection.

We later learned that his ritual hygiene and personal cleanliness routine was intended to teach us to keep clean and healthy during *'adverse conditions in the field'*.

Fire Piquet

The Fire Piquet was made up of either a junior officer or a SNCO and six guardsmen who were put on stand-by for 24 hours. The Piquet spent the night in the Guardroom but carried out normal duties by day. On mounting, the Fire Piquet Standing Orders outlining the duty was read out.

Immediate Action One

'As soon as the Duty Drummer sounds the Piquet bugle call you will without delay assemble at the specified location. Then having answered your name at the roll call you will man the fire-fighting equipment. This comprises a two-wheeled wooden hand cart, lengths of canvas hose, sand filled fire buckets, foam fire extinguishers, stirrup pumps and buckets, wooden fire beating brooms and fire resistant blankets. You will then receive instructions.'

Immediate Action Two

'On detecting a fire you will shout loudly, "Fire, Fire, Fire!" and urgently report the source by telephone or word of mouth to a responsible person.'

'If the fire is rated serious the Pioneer Sergeant will attend with the fire engine.'

Advisory note

'As a guardsman not being a trained firefighter you must not put yourself at risk by attempting to fight a fire. You must comply with orders given by the Officer i/c the Piquet.'

The Stirrup Pump widely used during the Second Word War comprised a portable hand-operated water pump with a footrest resembling a stirrup. It could be used only to extinguish small fires and was thought to be virtually useless.

The CO's prized lawn incident

Some years later when I was responsible for mowing the Commanding Officer's immaculately kept lawn I caused the Piquet to be called out. On that morning there was to be held a Battalion Drill Parade supervised by the Regimental Sergeant Major. To avoid participating in the parade I was 'on duty' mowing the lawn that extended from the Officers' Mess in Victoria Barracks, Windsor to the square. There was a tarmac road around the perimeter with a large flat area fronting the Officers' Mess used by WO2 Drill Sergeants when drilling officers.

Before the parade assembled I mounted the sit-on mower and commenced mowing close to the square. To and fro I went parallel to the square when as I was driving past him suddenly I heard the stentorian voice of the RSM bawling, 'Fuck off out of here.' The RSM was ready to give the battalion the order 'Get on parade' and I'd obviously seriously irritated him. I wasted no time driving up the centre of the lawn toward the furthest point, the Officers' Mess. Luck was not with me for after mowing to and fro once more I heard the scream of the Drill Sergeant who was taking officers on sword drill. 'Bugger off.' This I did without delay and drove to the central area where I started mowing a hollow square pattern. All went well until it began to pour with rain. That stopped the mowing. Couldn't mow in the rain so I parked the mower.

Next thing I knew was a message to me from the Piquet Officer ordering me to join him and the Piquet that he had sounded for. I reported to the young ensign and he said, 'What a mess you've made of the lawn. The CO will do his nut when he's on his daily walkabout. Then turning to the Piquet he ordered them to sweep the lawn with besom brooms made of a bundle of twigs tied to a stout handle, hoping to disguise the disorderly tracks criss-crossing the prized lawn. But the untidy appearance soon caught the CO's eye thereby displeasing him and resulting in the RSM gripping me, 'You're on a charge. Mowing the lawn in an irregular manner!' Next day on Company Orders, 'March in. Blah blah blah. Admonished. March out.'

3

Shining parade

Special attention was placed on uniform and kit during basic training as part of the 'bull' concept. 'Bulling' took up a lot of time. It was however a key part of recruit training that would help transform civilians into soldiers.

Best and second best uniforms had to be immaculately pressed and this was achieved either by covering the cloth with paper and applying a hot iron or carefully laying it out beneath the bottom sheet and sleeping on it. Steam irons were not available then so ironing presented a risk of scorching the item. Some recruits applied soap to the inside of the creases of the thick woollen trousers and added weights just above the anklets to give a smart appearance when on parade.

The butt of the .303 Lee Enfield rifle had to be highly polished and the working parts thoroughly cleaned, oiled and kept free of rust. Barrels were maintained to standard by slowly drawing squares of oily 4 x 2 cotton attached to a weighted brass 'pull-through' and cord through the entire length. Knowing that severe punishment would result should rust be detected during an inspection ensured that their personal weapon would be in perfect condition.

Blanco

A form of blanco was used by soldiers of the Empire from 1880 onwards. First adopted by the British Army to whiten buckskin leather equipment it was still used in the mid to late 20th Century. Guards Regiments used it to renovate their white buff belts and bayonet frogs worn with their Scarlet Tunics and Bearskins.

Blanco was widely used throughout both First and Second World Wars as a cleaning and colouring compound. Most infantry units used a shade of green. The Royal Armoured Corps used black. Airforce units used RAF blue and the RMP 'Snowdrops' and Royal Navy white.

But before ending up in Egypt, no doubt many recruits may recall going to the NAAFI or PRI in UK and grudgingly spending their limited pay on cylindrical blocks of hard green 'Blanco' tins of metal polish and yellow dusters.

Each evening recruits had to endure a two-hour shining parade. Sitting silently on their bed as no talking or smoking was permitted, they applied blanco with a dampened brush and rubbed it into the their webbing: belt and anklets, bayonet frog, field service marching order (FSMO) - comprising ammo pouches, webbing and small pack and also their big pack. Then followed the struggle to clear surplus blanco and polish the brass buckles. Cap star, buttons and ammo boots were polished to glistering perfection. Although after a while recruits managed to transform the whiteish natural coloured kit issued to a reasonable standard of green it had to be done over and over again each evening.

At 2130 hours the Superintending Sergeant inspected everything to ensure that it was in immaculate condition. If it wasn't to his liking, out of the window went the green blanket with all the kit laid out for inspection. Evil b------!

Later while in the Canal Zone for some there was still no escape from the blanco and metal polish routine. Winter guard mounting, drill parades and standard turnout still demanded never-ending bull.

But years later the phasing out of cotton webbing and introduction of 'Staybright' buttons made the use of Blanco,and Bluebell metal polish redundant. What a relief! But how could old soldiers ever forget the cylindrical metal tin with screw cap and its picture of a bluebell flower with five flower heads in front of a circular yellow background?

4
Square bashing

'Drill makes a soldier disciplined and teaches them to take a pride in their appearance and manner', announced the Superintending Sergeant when he arrived to induct our squad to the contents of the Brigade of Guards drill book.

Inspections

Every parade was preceded by an arduous inspection by either our L/Cpl Drill Instructor or the fearsome Supervising Sergeant who'd inspect every detail of our uniform, personal appearance and bearing. Failing his inspection for any reason, no matter how small would be sure to result in punishment. From Day One we'd learned that he couldn't 'stand a dirty guardsman'.

But what constituted a dirty guardsman? To him the slightest speck of dust, polish residue on brasses, a grimy fingernail, bum-fluff on the chin or any other imperfection in turnout would fit his perception of 'filth'.

After a few weeks of square-bashing an inspection by the Superintending Sergeant was due. The squad fell in forming three perfectly dressed ranks. Then could be heard rapid 'click clacks', the sound of the heels of metal tipped boots striking the square. 'It's him', we whispered as the approaching steps got nearer and the clacks louder.

'Squad. Squad shun', screamed the L/Cpl Squad Instructor standing to attention. Followed by 'Squad present and ready for your inspection Sergeant.'

The ordeal had begun. Majestically the sadist, wearing his red sash, strode along the front rank with blue eyes glaring at each recruit, seeking out their imperfections. 'What's that?' Followed by the sound of a dull thud and a grunt as wooden pace stick was rammed into the stomach of the first victim.

'Pull your guts in and stick your chest out. You look like a pregnant woman!'

A few more paces and it was my turn. I'd fallen victim of his scrutiny. Several days earlier I was shaving with my dead sharp Rolls Razor when the bloke next to me lunged into me causing the razor to cut my top lip. It was quite a deep cut and bled profusely before stopping and leaving a nasty little wound. So for the next few days I didn't shave the top lip fearing that I'd re-open the cut. This resulted in a short black growth of bristles on the upper lip.

'What's that fungus on your top lip?'

'I cut myself. I'm growing a moustache Sergeant.'

'Well get a fucking move on it!'

Moving on. 'Dirty cap star. Show clean tonight.'

'Dirty chinstrap brasses.'

'Crack!' Followed by stifled moan as pace stick struck knuckles.

'Curl your fingers up and turn your wrist in. Thumbs in-line with the seam of your trousers. You idle sod!'

Having completed his inspection and decided that what he had seen didn't meet his expectations he turned to the L/Cpl Instructor and said, 'They're a bloody shower! I'm going to get a move on them.'

'Right. You are going to march and keep marching smartly until I halt you. On the command "quick march" step forward 30 inches with your left foot and continue marching keeping your head and eyes fixed to the front.

'Swing your arms nine inches straight to the front and six inches straight to the rear without bending them at your elbow. Keep your fingers curled up. Or you'll feel my pace stick.'

'We're in for a chasing. He'll keep us going until we drop.'

'Move to the right in three's. By the left quick march left, right, left...', he shouted upping the step to well over 140 per minute. 'About turn,' he repeatedly ordered ignoring our obvious discomfort until he finally relented and gave the order, 'Squad halt.'

Gasping for breath the squad stood silently until suddenly a recruit coughed loudly. This was our tormentor's chance to get in among us.

Confronting the victim who'd coughed we heard the Sergeant say,

'Have you got consumption?'

'No sergeant,' the recruit breathlessly whispered.

'I'd be chuffed to fuck if you have. You'd die a horrible death.'

Seemingly satisfied he handed over to our Drill Instructor and strutted off.

We felt that the descriptor 'sadist' fitted him well. In our simplistic view of the world at the time it seemed to us that he gained immense pleasure from the infliction of pain and mental suffering. But under his leadership we succeeded and what he taught us would serve us well throughout our lifetime.

In truth this man was a giant who loved the Regiment and all that it stood for. He was the source of our properly disciplined life and gave us confidence in whatever we did. He was revered by all whom he trained and worked with. Possibly a descendent of one of the Welshmen of 24th of Foot defending Rorke's Drift during the Zulu War he ranks among the finest of sergeants. A legend who certainly delivered the *Nulli Secundus* concept, he was Sgt Rhondda Collins, who is thought by some Coldstreamers to be on duty in Paradise with orders to 'march in' newcomers passing through the Narrow Gate and direct 'wasters' to the Broad Gate through which those not up to scratch pass.

Typical drills

Some of the drills learned by the author 66 years ago are described below. Obviously with the passage of time memories may become flawed. So I'll ask those readers who are or have been drill instructors to bear with me and make allowances for lapses of memory or incorrect descriptors. For the content may well differ from the authorised Drill Book.

Our Drill Instructor always began with a brief description of the drill movement followed by; 'Watch me and I'll give you a complete demonstration with key points to note explained.' Then followed instructions such as the following examples.

Fall-in

'Form three ranks on the right marker. Dressing, 'right dress', Right Marker stand still. You two behind him raise your arm to your front to get the correct spacing between ranks. Remainder of the front rank raise your right arm parallel to the ground and touch the shoulder of the man next to you. Then everyone except the right-hand men look right and shuffle your feet until you're perfectly aligned.'

Stand easy

'Stand with your feet apart. Relax. Don't talk or move your feet about.'

Stand at ease

'Raise your left leg and stamp it down leaving your feet twelve inches apart. Brace both your arms behind your back. Lock your hands. When holding your rifle keep your right arm at the side of your body NOT behind it.'

Attention (shun)

'Raise the left leg up so that the thigh is parallel to the ground and bring down the left boot sharply. Legs straight, wrist turned in, thumbs in line with seam of trousers, look up at centre of the cap of man in front, heels together toes 45 degrees apart. Weight on balls of feet.'

Foot drill at the halt

Right turn

'This movement will enable you to turn through an angle of 90 degrees to the right. Swivel your right foot 90 degrees to the right. Raise your left foot and stamp it down next to your right boot. Count the time 1-2 3-1.'

About turn

'You will turn 180 degrees clockwise ending up facing the opposite direction. On the command "About turn" swivel to your right. Always to the right. Bring your left boot down smartly. Feet at 45 degrees. Count the time. One, two three One.'

Open order march

'On the command "Open order march" front rank step forward, rear rank backward to open up the ranks. Then get your dressing. On the command "Close order march" you'll resume the original spacing. We'll also cover "Form two ranks" and "Form three ranks" and we'll do these drills until you get it perfect!'

Saluting

'Salute to the front you will pull your feet in and salute counting "Up two three down". Straight forearm with hand correctly positioned. Between salutes adopt position of attention. Wrist turned in. Right turn. Away.'

Foot drill on the march

Drill Instructor says, 'Most commands I'll give whilst you're marching will be when your left heel hits the ground. You'll get advance warning known as a "cautionary command" followed by the "execute command" which is when you carry out the order.'

Quick march

'Right Marker fix your eye on a distant object. When I give the order "By the right quick march" step off on the left foot. Left, right, left...'

Change step

'This is the drill when you need to get back in step. Left, left, right....'

'Oh dear what a muddle.'

Halt

'Pull your feet in - check one-two.'

'Sod it. I've scraped the polish of my left heel. Should have been more careful when I slammed my right boot down.'

About turn

'You'll turn 180 degrees to the right, ending up facing the opposite direction. Watch me and I'll give you a complete demonstration! I'll give the command "About turn" as your right heel strikes the ground. Then take a check pace with the left foot. Move your right foot to the instep of the left foot. Raise your left knee while the right foot pivots your body 90 degrees to the right. Raise the right knee while your left pivots 90 degrees to the right. That brings your body to face 180 degrees. The left knee is raised and lowered to complete the movement. Then step off with your right foot. Count out the movements, "Check, in 1,2,3, forward" left right left...'

'Oh dear confusion! What a muddle!'

Right wheel

'The squad will pivot about the Right Marker who'll edge slowly to his right while the rest of you move round by 90 degrees. Step short on the right, step out on the left.'

Mark time

'Arms in. Knees up. Left, right, left...' Speed picking up. Racing now.

'Slow down you halfwits!'

Eyes right

'Right Marker eyes front and look where you're going. The others turn your head to the right until you get the order "eyes front". Then face forward.'

'Oh dear we're wobbling about all over the place.'

Saluting

'Salute to the front salute. March toward the officer. Halt and give two salutes. About turn. March off in the opposite direction. Count the time. "Up two three down two three up two three down." Brace your arm back. Keep your f......g wrist straight and don't curl your little finger up.'

Double sentry

Two sentries are posted at selected points where they are to guard the post. As they will be on duty for two hours they'll need to stretch their legs after standing at ease for some time. So at a given signal they will both spring to attention, slope arms and begin to march to and fro until they stop.

Members of the public scratch their heads wondering how the two sentries synchronise their movements. Do they have some kind of miniature radio hidden within their bearskins? 'No, it's simple; they have a recognised code signalled by rifle-butt taps of the senior guardsman at each post.' One tap means patrol; two taps salute and three taps present arms. To stop patrolling the senior guardsman extends the index finger of his left hand.

Slow march

'Bring your foot forward and point it downwards and outwards. Hold it just above the ground briefly then slide it onto the ground. "By the right slow march" left, right. Keep your balance. Stop wobbling about.'

Arms drill

Samples of the drills taught are outlined below.

Slope arms

'Raise your rifle to the slope on your left shoulder. Magazine facing to the left. Support it with your left arm at an angle of ninety degrees.'

Order arms

'Your rifle will be held vertically on the right side with the butt on the ground.'

Bayonet drill

'Squad will fix bayonets. Bayonets. Fix. Shun!' Followed by the clatter of bayonets dropping to ground.

'Oh dear.' A severe reprimand follows.

Present arms

'Bring your rifle to the front centre of your bodies and place your right foot behind your left. When presenting arms hold position until order given to slope arms. I'll demonstrate the movements now.'

Port arms

'You'll need to learn how to Port Arms and also the Outward Turn. You'll start from the "Order Arms" position. On the command "Port Arms" you will grasp your rifle barrel with your right hand and move the rifle diagonally across your body. Count "two three" then with the left hand grasp the trigger guard keeping the rifle close to your waist. Count "two three" and grasp the rifle at the stock with your right hand. Stand still and continue to hold the rifle diagonally across your body. You'll need to port arms when presenting your weapon for inspection and clearing springs during weapon training.'

Outward turn

'Right. A bit of history for you. Your Regiment's colours embody its spirit and service as well as its fallen guardsmen. For centuries the loss of a colour was considered the greatest shame on a battlefield, consequently our Regimental colours are venerated by officers and guardsmen of all ranks.'

'With luck one day you'll take part in the "Trooping the Colour Ceremony". On battlefields regimental colours were used as rallying points. Ensigns slowly marched with their colours between the ranks of guardsmen to enable them to recognise their Regiment's colours.'

'Today to the first six bars of "God Save the Queen", the Escort to the Colour presents arms. Simultaneously the NCOs at the four corners of the Escort port arms turning outward at an angle of 45 degrees as symbolic maximum protection for the colour. I'll demonstrate the drill now.'

Change arms

'Move your rifle from left shoulder to right...'

More advanced drills such as ceremonial and funeral drills were taught towards the end of the drill course.

5

The Guards Training Battalion at Pirbright

After 16 weeks of recruit basic training in the form of square-bashing, physical training, muscle strengthening exercises and fatigues, a truly gruelling and frightful experience, I passed the programme and moved to Pirbright Camp in Surrey. There we were accommodated in draughty huts called 'spiders'.

Then followed 12 weeks of weapon training and tactics that while not exactly up to SAS standards was pretty grim. Stripping, assembling and firing the trusty .303 Lee Enfield rifle, Bren gun, Sten gun that easily jammed, PIAT (projectile infantry anti-tank) weapon that when fired gave us headaches and deafened us, 2" Mortars, grenades etc. Quite different to todays sophisticated weapons.

We then moved on to personal camouflage and concealment and practised fieldcraft in order to introduce us to the means by which we could survive by being less conspicuous. We learned to conceal ourselves making the best use of cover without restricting our field of view.

How to move stealthily using the terrain wherever possible to mask our movements or provide shelter from enemy fire was stressed as was peeping around a wall or gate rather than exposing oneself by looking over the top. These and many other logical things were covered.

By applying camouflage cream we blackened our faces. We changed the shape of our helmets by stuffing bracken and gorse into the nets covering them and anywhere we could in the Field Service Marching Order (FSMO). This included web belt, bayonet frog, braces, ammo pouches, water bottle and small pack.

We prepared defensive positions by 'digging in' using short steel entrenching tools to create slit trenches and shell scrapes. Security was by means of setting up trip wires, explosives (thunder flashes) and warning devices.

The fieldcraft tactical exercises involved either occupying good static defensive firing positions or conducting platoon attacks moving forward in formations such as 'Blobs One Up' with a single 'section' deployed forward. Or 'Blobs 2 or 3 Up' where two or three sections advanced.

'Pepper-potting' was quite enjoyable. It involved individuals getting up randomly and firing rounds in a chaotic advance.

Bayonet charging was a laugh. Having attached our 'pig sticker' bayonets, urged on by our instructors, we rushed toward sacks stuffed with straw screaming loudly and stabbing furiously at the sacks.

Live grenade throwing drills were not pleasant and all prayed that nobody would drop one even though they had long fuses.

Staggering around in gas masks and exposure to tear gas was unpleasant but a necessary skill to be endured.

On one occasion after dark we were marched to the ranges and halted at a point 1000 yards from the targets. We were then instructed to observe the path alongside the range where at a given signal someone standing on the track lit up a cigarette to illustrate the danger of smoking in the open at night. Yes, we learned how clearly the red tip of a lighted fag could be seen from a considerable distance putting others at risk.

We also learned how to work as a team while patrolling at night and practised the 'ghost walk'. This involved moving silently and carefully lifting one's feet up to clear hidden booby trap trip wires while slowly waving arms around and above the body. The 'monkey run' was another seemingly senseless activity.

Target practice on the range proved to be an ordeal. Normal live firing practice was OK but the final session involved moving rapidly progressing in 200-yard increments from the 1000-yard point and firing 10 rounds application aimed at 6 feet targets. But at the final 200 yard point we were ordered to reload, fix bayonets, run 100 yards, stop and discharge 10 rounds rapid fire at the target. What a disaster that was! We were so exhausted and breathless that to stand upright and fire with our rifles now describing uncontrollable circles we were lucky to hit any part of the target!

An assortment of survival skills was taught at Pirbright that came in handy later during battle training at Pickering.

Being only 5' 9" tall and weighing only 130 pounds I was at a disadvantage when confronting the required test: recovering a much heavier wounded casualty by 'fireman carry' within a specified time limit.

Tackling an obstacle course was challenging. It comprised rope climbing, crossing terrain by rope ladders, scrambling over 8 foot walls, forming a pyramid enabling others to reach the top and drop over the other side then pulling up the pyramid team; leaping down into sand pits and water, crawling through hollow pipes.

Possibly the worst bit was struggling face up under barbed wire amidst live firing with coloured smoke bombs and thunder flashes exploding all around.

We also learned to cross barbed wire entanglements by getting one man to lie on top of the wire so as to flatten it while the squad stepped on his body to cross the wire. We also used wire cutters proficiently avoiding the ends of the wire flying about.

After attaining the required level of skills we spent two weeks battle training on the Yorkshire Moors at Pickering. This involved forced marches with rifle and packs and I remember the platoon getting puffed out while marching uphill. We were gasping for breath.

'Step short you buggers. Sing or double!' shouted 'Legs' McKenna, our Platoon Sergeant.

What agony.

Constructing a shelter in the field presented a bit of a problem. All we had was our Poncho Capes, entrenching tool and what we stood up in. But there were trees, rocks to anchor the cape, branches and stuff about that we could make use of.

I dug a shallow 'grave' and part-filled it with leaves and formed a kind of teepee above it with fallen timber. Then I draped my Poncho over it facing the wind direction and secured the base with rocks hoping that it wouldn't rain when I lay down in the depression. Job done.

Initiative testing was something I'd never forget. The platoon boarded a 3-ton Bedford truck that transported us into the depths of the Yorkshire Moors. It stopped and we got off and fell-in. An officer got out of the cab and gave us verbal instructions before issuing us with a written list of objectives and items to be obtained without expending any money. Then we were despatched each in a different direction tasked with a set of targets to achieve.

Truthfully I cannot recall any of the items on my listing other than the one instructing me to obtain a 'bun penny'. I was close to a small village bakery shop and went in to scrounge a penny bun for free. I explained that I wasn't allowed to buy one and being in uniform the kindly woman serving took pity on me and gave me a current bun. I was well pleased and struck that off my list.

After joining others on their way back to the pick-up point and going round and round in circles due to lack of understanding of contour lines etc. we caught sight of the truck and headed for it.

On reaching the assembly area at conclusion of the test I was debriefed by an officer to whom I proudly presented the bun.

'Oh. Oh. Oh! You idiot. Don't you know what a Bun Penny is?'

'No Sir. Isn't this good enough?'

'No. A Bun Penny is a coin featuring the young Queen Victoria. It was so called as she had her hair arranged in a bun. No marks for that task.'

On completion we returned to Pirbright for the final week's training

Miraculously I'd managed to pass out as a fully trained guardsman.

6

Posting to the 1st Battalion at Windsor

What a relief it was when in June 1951 I was posted to No. 3 Company of the 1st Battalion Coldstream Guards stationed in Victoria Barracks, Windsor. Our transport stopped outside the RSM's office and we the newly posted young guardsmen climbed down from the truck. Forming a group we stood to attention and awaited WO1 (RSM) Robert William 'Dusty' Smith MBE DCM who soon appeared.

Speaking quite normally without screaming or shouting he greeted the newcomers with, 'Good morning. Stand at ease. Welcome to the 1st Battalion.' after which he gave us a short pep talk outlining what he expected of us. Then before dismissing the group he turned to me, the shortest man, placed a large firm hand on my shoulder and said, 'You're only little but remember you're as good as these big fellows. You've shown that you can hack it. Never forget that.' He then dismissed us and returned to his office leaving me feeling good.

Ready for first Victoria Barracks Guard duty

Having been inducted to No. 3 Company, other than barrack guards outside the Guardroom at the gate facing Sheep Street, I spent most of my short time with the Company on drill parades and fatigues.

The photograph reproduced above shows the author sporting a moustache standing on the left with two of his squad mates from the Guards Depot days.

During the autumn of 1951 the Battalion went on exercise on Salisbury Plain and fortunately for me I didn't have to dig slit trenches or 'stand-to' in ankle-deep water as having trained as a civilian heavy goods (LGV) mechanic and licensed truck driver I'd been temporarily attached to the MT Platoon. Throughout the exercise each night I slept in my No. 3 Company 15 cwt. Fordson baggage truck, as did Company Sergeant Major (CSM) '*Geordie*' Reid. After the exercises Captain FWR Fisher, the MT Officer, retained me and that's how I got involved with the MT.

7

THE 1ST BATTALION COLDSTREAM GUARDS MOVES FROM WINDSOR TO THE CANAL ZONE VIA CYPRUS

Deployment to Cyprus

In mid-October 1951 the 1st Battalion was put on 28 days notice to move to Cyprus as a unit of the 32nd Guards Brigade. Then on the 22nd November 1951, less than a year after the 1st Battalion had returned from a tour in Tripoli, it marched out of Victoria Barracks and entrained at Windsor for Portsmouth. There the Battalion paraded in 'Greatcoat Order' in front of HMS *Victory* before boarding.

1st Battalion Coldstream Guards formed up at Portsmouth Docks

HMS Illustrious at sea

The troops were to board the aircraft carrier HMS *Illustrious* to be transported to Cyprus. The main hanger had been strung with 1500 hammocks in order to accommodate the troops.

Main hanger strung with 1500 hammocks

On 19 November dockers began loading our transport and large items of equipment onto the flight deck.

Loading transport

Transport loaded on the flight deck

Illustrious set sail on 23rd November 1951 arriving at Famagusta on the 29th. On board with us were the 1st Battalion Bedfordshire & Hertfordshire Regiment, the 45th Field Regiment Royal Artillery and other units of 3rd Infantry Division. The third battalion comprising 32nd Guards Brigade was the 1st Battalion Scots Guards based in Nicosia.

The 39th Infantry Brigade also part of 3rd Inf. Div. comprising the 1st Battalion Royal East Kent Regiment (the Buffs) and the 1st Battalion Royal Inniskilling Fusiliers had sailed on her earlier, reaching Famagusta on 11th November. So the crew were well versed in troop transport. The 1st Battalion Border Regiment joined later to complete the 39th Brigade that on leaving Cyprus like the 32nd were to take up duties in the Canal Zone.

The Bay of Biscay was very rough and the sea broke over the bows as the ship ploughed through the waves.

Rough seas in the Bay of Biscay

We dropped anchor outside Gibraltar Harbour while a guardsman who'd been operated on for appendicitis by the ship's medical staff was landed. The photograph shows the aircraft lift open. This was done because it got so hot below deck.

HMS Illustrious anchored off Gibraltar

Sick man being hoisted off the ship

Disembarking at Famagusta, Cyprus

HMS *Illustrious* docked in Famagusta Harbour in Cyprus on 29 November 1951 where the troops disembarked. Troops were offloaded onto rather dangerous looking flat-decked lighters, the *Illustrious* being too large to dock at the quayside. I was not a happy bunny, as we were crowded onto the vessels wearing greatcoats and laden with full kit, blankets and rifle. An accidental shove could easily have sent some unfortunate overboard to the bottom, but thankfully we all made it.

In pouring rain an assortment of local trucks fitted out as crude 'buses' with wooden benches and canvas window flaps carried the Battalion to Polemedhia Camp located on a hillside above Limassol. It was pouring with rain (as it did for the next two months) while we struggled up the hill to collect mattresses and bedding for our tents. The Battalion remained there presumably standing-by until needed either locally or in the Canal Zone.

Polemedia Camp

Sgt George Clack a 'Dead Regimental Coldstreamer'

I'd like to record fond memories of my former boss and friend George Clack when he was MT Sergeant of the1st Battalion Coldstream Guards. It's difficult to know where to start this tribute to George for when I first met him he was a capable long-serving and 'dead regimental' Coldstreamer Sergeant, whereas I was a young guardsman when I joined his platoon in UK. He did however know that whilst in No. 3 Company I'd taken a military Trade Test at 10 Command Workshops, REME, Mill Hill, London, where I'd passed as Vehicle Mechanic Class III with 'A' Grade and that I held a full driving licence. That's about all.

Having collected our unit trucks they were used to cover the daily logistic runs, troop transport and load carrying for the Quartermaster staff. Our regular routes were from Polemedia Camp to and from Limassol, Larnaca, Famagusta, the Troodos mountains area and Nicosia.

Guardsman Norman Smith did the daily mail run to Nicosia and thereby hangs a tale. There was to be a vehicle inspection on a given day and that day on his return from Nicosia he lifted his Land Rover bonnet and sprayed petrol from his fire extinguisher onto the engine hoping to clean up inaccessible places. Unfortunately he set the Land Rover ablaze and also Captain Towers' new Ford Consul saloon that was parked in the garage next to Smith's Land Rover. Wow! What a mess. Poor old Smith N. Soon afterwards the following poem appeared on the MT Notice Board:

Guardsman Smith N. usually thick
Can send a Land Rover up in a tick
On red-hot engine he does flick
POL till the flames do lick...

(Sorry, but I cannot recall the rest of the poem)

I remember driving my truck on details in Cyprus. It was the 15 cwt. Fordson V8 WOT 2 I'd driven on the Salisbury Plain exercises. I took the photograph reproduced below when on the way back to Polemedia Camp I'd stopped to watch the camels feeding on trees by the roadside.

Camels grazing on roadside trees

It was not a good day as I'd been booked by the RMPs for failing to immobilise my truck outside a roadside cafe where the Pioneer Sergeant with me asked me to stop for a brew. What a silly boy, all I needed to do was remove the rotor arm and I'd have avoided the charge sheet that would be sure to end up on my Commanding Officer's Desk. It did and I received extra drills for punishment.

Then one day I was ordered to the MT Office to understudy L/Sgt 'Kipper' Adams, a good-looking bloke who smoked a lot and was nearing his discharge date. He was the MT Clerk working under George's supervision. I didn't know what to make of George because he was rather regimental and young soldiers like me were very wary of Full Sergeants sporting their red infantry sashes – and George always always wore his sash.

I took to the work and became very interested in the paperwork and procedures to be maintained. L/Sgt Adams was a patient and good teacher and I learned quickly. George, of course, knew it all and was always a very busy man who made the key decisions.

8

The Cyprus troubles 1950 onwards

The author often wondered why his unit, the 1st Battalion Coldstream Guards, was deployed to Cyprus in a bit of a hurry and decided to look back at the events there in the 1950s. Was the hurried posting because HM Government could foresee terrorist trouble there or was it simply a holding base until the 32nd Guards Brigade and others were to be sent to Egypt?

Cyprus troubles -the troublemaker Archbishop Makarios III

The son of a shepherd, Michail Christodoulou Mouskos Makarios was born in 1913. At the age of 33 he was ordained as a priest and in 1946 he left Cyprus to study at an American University. That is where he earned his reputation as a keen promoter of Enosis (a Greek term describing the Greek Cypriot movement for political union with Greece) and met really wealthy American Greeks who financed his campaigns in Cyprus.

In 1950 aged 37 he was elected Archbishop of Cyprus and became a popular figure among Greek Cypriots, probably due to his vigorous support for Enosis. This disturbed the Turkish Cypriot minority and eventually led to the 1974 invasion by Turkish Forces and partition.

Lt Col George Grivas

George Grivas a fanatical Enotist and Greek nationalist born in 1898 was promoted while serving with 2nd Athens Division during the 2nd World War. He was determined to drive the British out of Cyprus and planned and executed a guerilla campaign to achieve his goal.

He and Makarios first met in July 1951 and together they discussed the best means of gaining public support for Enosis. While Lt Col Grivas was dead set on employing terrorism and violent means to achieve his aims, Makarios wasn't keen on armed conflict. But in 1952, probably influenced by the unyielding position adopted by Anthony Eden the British Foreign Secretary earlier in November 1951, Makarios became chairman of Lt Col Grivas's revolutionary committee based in Athens.

The Turkish Cypriot view

In the late 1950s, the Turkish Cypriots proposed Taksim (partition), as a reaction to the Greek ideal of Enosis; feeling that they would be persecuted in a Greek-dominated Cyprus. They thought that only by keeping part of the island under either British or Turkish sovereignty could their safety be guaranteed. This led the Cyprus dispute to become increasingly polarised, causing the two communities to adopt extreme opposing positions with conflicting perceptions of the future of the island.

In August 1954 Greece, no doubt prompted by Makarios, raised the question of Cyprus at the United Nations, proposing that the principle of self-determination (Enosis) be applied to Cyprus. This led Turkey to become mindful of the risks to its own security as well as the safety of Turkish citizens in Cyprus. The Turks feared that if Cyprus joined Greece and a communist government took over in Athens, a Russian-Greek alliance could use the island for hostile purposes.

The British position

On 28 July 1954 Eden declared the British position, saying that due to demands from the Egyptian President Gamal Abdel Nasser, Britain had agreed to evacuate the Suez Canal base commencing October 1954 to be completed by 18 July 1956. Eden added that Britain would be transferring her Middle East military headquarters to Cyprus. So for strategic reasons, Britain was intent on maintaining a military presence on the island.

The British Government however was afraid that concessions over Cyprus would be seen as a sign of weakness by Arab countries and would offend Turkey. So having agreed to leave the Canal Zone, the British Government didn't wish to evacuate Cyprus, it being an ideal base for operations covering the eastern Mediterranean and the Middle East. Furthermore, Britain needed to keep their base in Cyprus to fulfil treaty obligations with some Arab states, NATO and the United Nations.

In November 1954, Lt Col Grivas arrived secretly in Cyprus and in January 1955 he met Makarios in Larnaca. There he learned that the Athens Government was now fully sympathetic with their agreed aims. A pro-Enosis independence organisation EOKA (translated as the National Organization of Cypriot Fighters) was formed.

Greek-Cypriot frustrations erupted once more into violence. A general strike was called and vicious riots flared up between the Greek and

Turkish Cypriots. The greatly increased unrest enabled Lt Col Grivas, a master of guerrilla warfare, to launch his terrorist campaign against British Rule and between the two Cypriot communities.

The EOKA operatives were superbly trained in arts of sabotage, ambush and execution and their bomb attacks all over the island wrecked government offices, police stations and military installations. They even blew up the radio transmitter in Nicosia as bomb attacks swept the island. No one felt safe and things got so bad that a state of emergency was declared, enabling detention without trial and the death penalty for unauthorised possession of weapons and explosives. The British Government was now facing a nationwide Cypriot rebellion.

Greece submits a United Nations resolution

On 20 August 1955, Greece submitted a petition to the UN requesting self-determination for the people of Cyprus. After that, the colonial government of Cyprus enforced the anti-sedition laws for the purpose of preventing or suppressing demonstrations in favour of union with Greece; but Makarios continued demanding self-determination for Cyprus.

In October 1955, with the security situation deteriorating, the British Governor opened talks on the island's future. By now, Makarios was closely identified with the insurgency and talks broke up without any agreement.

Suppressing the terrorists

To deal with the terrorists HM Forces were called up. The British Army responded quickly and forcefully with riot control, weapons searches and patrols and from the beginning of 1955 to the end of 1959 fought against EOKA. Armoured vehicles were often used, mainly on hard roads, but trucks didn't move after dark except when absolutely necessary. The risk of ambush was ever present because Lt Col Grivas's terrorists conducted a mini war of fast movement. They always appeared when least expected and were secretly supported by Enosis collaborators.

To deal with about 2 000 detained suspected EOKA terrorists, the Royal Engineers constructed notorious well-guarded 'detention' camps (or concentration camps one might suspect). Located in remote areas the camps comprised basic wooden huts within razor wire pens. Greek media labelled them 'Britain's Belsens'.

Hastings aircraft fly the 1st Battalion Gordon Highlanders into Nicosia

The following report outlines the kind of conflict our forces needed to confront.

'In the autumn of 1955, 1st Battalion The Gordon Highlanders was on leave in the United Kingdom. Recalled at 48 hours notice, they were the first British Army Unit since 1945 to fly out to an Emergency.

Landing in Cyprus in October, the Battalion Headquarters and 'A' and 'B' Companies were based around Xeros, with a large camp being eventually formed named Aberdeen. 'C' and 'D' Companies were sent to the Troodos Mountains.

The Gordon's two main aims were to improve security and to obtain information. Road and coastal patrols were carried out; roadblocks were set up police stations guarded and house-to-house searches made, often on a large scale. In mid November 1955, EOKA launched widespread attacks throughout the island including the use of bombs. The unrest even spread to schools where action was required to quell the disturbances. An official State of Emergency was declared but EOKA terrorists continued their campaign of killing both soldiers and civilians. The Gordon's carried out routine patrols, localised searches and more extended operations into 1956. Numbers of terrorists were captured. EOKA distributed leaflets accusing British Troops of using Nazi German Gestapo police tactics.'

Source: www.rememberingscotlandatwar.org.uk

Makarios exiled

During March 1956 due to his obstinacy and continual demands for self-determination he was intercepted by Special Branch officers while boarding a flight at Nicosia airport. This resulted in Makarios being exiled to an island in the Seychelles, as a 'guest' of the Governor of the Seychelles.

He was released from exile after a year and forbidden to return to Cyprus; so he went to Athens where he continued working for Enosis.

Makarios returns to Cyprus

On 01 March 1959 Makartios returned to Nicosia where almost two-thirds of the adult Greek Cypriot population turned out to welcome him. Presidential elections were held on 13 December 1959, resulting in Makarios becoming the First President of the Republic of Cyprus and political leader of all Cyprus. He also became leader of the Greek Cypriot community.

Makarios' political aims mirrored those of Lt Col George Grivas, however in later life he categorically denied any involvement in the violent resistance undertaken by EOKA. But various conflicts took place there for many years after these events.

From the beginning of 1955 to the end of 1959 HM Forces fought against EOKA although that probably didn't affect too many servicemen and women who'd served in the Canal Zone of Egypt. But either a General Service Medal or a Cyprus Clasp was issued to those who served there between 1st April 1955 and 18th April 1959 during the terrorist troubles.

9

THE 1ST BATTALION MOVES TO EGYPT

Riots in Egypt

In mid-January 1952 came reports of agitation against the British leading to violent rioting in Cairo and murders as the situation in Egypt worsened. Apparently plans were made for the Coldstream Guards to conduct assault landings on the Alexandria beaches to restore order and protect the European population but subsequently shelved.

On 6th February 1952, the morning the BBC announced the death of King George VI; the 1st Battalion left Cyprus aboard the *Empire Doric* bound for Port Said. So the Regiment played no part in the Cyprus troubles outlined above.

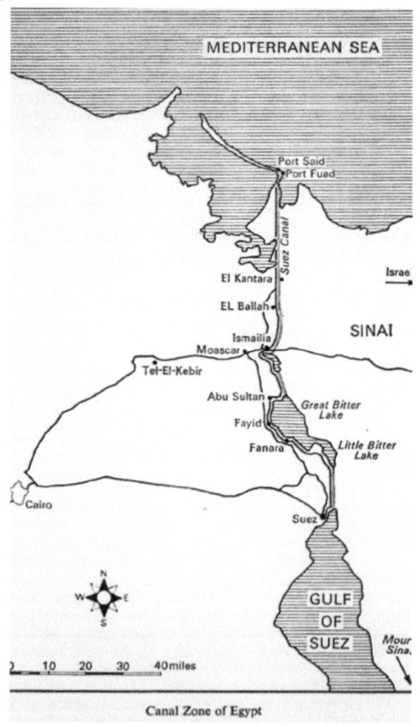

Map of Canal Zone 1951-1954

Deployment to Tel-el-Kebir

We docked in Port Said surrounded by a flotilla of bumboats whose occupants offered virtually everything for sale or barter.

The Battalion, having disembarked, was transported to St. Louis Camp that was located within the perimeter wire of Tel-el-Kebir (TEK) where it took up Garrison Duties. The men were accommodated in tents while some worked in old huts previously occupied by the Mauritian Pioneer Companies, so it was pretty basic. The Transport Officer drew up some 2nd World War Dodge 3 Ton Cargo trucks that were used for garbage collection and whatever tasks the MT were allotted. The 1st Battalion was also responsible with other units for perimeter defence, main gate guards, manning searchlights and mobile and foot patrols along the wire. But this didn't stop the Egyptian 'Klefti Wallah's' breaking-in and stealing anything of value.

The 1st Battalion moves to El Ballah

The Battalion wasn't in TEK very long, for on 17th February 1952 there was a 'change of quarter' order and it moved to Wolseley Camp, El Ballah.

The 1st Battalion sign - Wolseley Camp, El Ballah

Wolseley Camp was situated on the Treaty Road between El Kantara and Ismailia, lying between the so-called 'Sweet Water Canal' and the Suez Canal.

The Battalion was based there for about 18 months, surrounded on all sides by sand. Virtually nothing but sand. Huge black flies and blue-bottles plagued us by day and the dreaded mosquitoes at night. Boring, boring, boring. Guards, guards, guards day and night.

Local detachments

Responsibilities included a detachment sent to Port Fuad on the East Bank of the Suez Canal, another guarding the El Kantara ferry and fresh water pumping station while the Support Company Medium Machine Gun (MMG) platoon protected the track from the desert into El Ballah and El Kantara. The objective being to deter terrorists.

On one occasion I was deployed with a platoon to a location close to El Kantara with orders to *'Guard the approaches to Cairo.'*

Bivouacking near El Kantara

A curious intruder

We spent some time bivouacked there but didn't encounter any terrorists, only a few curious children, perhaps budding extremists.

The outlying companies and platoons were withdrawn in April 1952 so that the complete Battalion was located in Wolseley Camp, El Ballah. Its operational role continued to be the occupation of Alexandria if tasked to do so. Consequently, troop movements by air from Canal Zone airfields were practised.

Meanwhile the 1st Battalion continued its day-to-day existence in Wolseley Camp but was tasked with watching/guarding the El Kantara Ferry on the Port Said to Ismailia road about 30 km north of Ismailia.

It was also responsible for securing and protecting the El Firdan Railway Swing Bridge spanning the Suez Canal near Ismailia. Members of the guard detachment manned a tented outpost beside the Canal.

The 1st Battalion was often tasked with raiding villages near the Sweet Water Canal searching for stolen property, arms and suspected terrorists. Like the Paras and other units we operated anti-cable-cutting patrols in Land Rovers fitted with sturdy angle iron structures mounted vertically on the front bumpers to counter the 'wire across the road obstacles'. Terrorists stretched steel wire at head height across the roads intending to decapitate ill informed motor cyclists and drivers with their windscreens folded flat. An armed escort vehicle followed the patrols as ambushes and terrorist attacks frequently occurred. As readers will probably know, single vehicles weren't allowed to travel due to the inherent risks.

Water Filtration and Purification Plant Guard

The 1st Battalion was also tasked with guarding the nearby Water Filtration and Purification Plant. I recall being Sergeant of the Guard there quite often. We mounted night-guard in greatcoat order because it got so cold during the night, in contrast to the dusty intense heat of the day. Tall well-built Sudanese men armed with cudgels patrolled the depot all night long supporting the guard. My first order after scheduling duties was for all to get out and collect enough wood to burn throughout the night on the slow combustion stove. Once alight those not on 'stag' would cluster around the stove with the lid open intent on keeping warm. The Sudanese could get on with their patrolling whilst we hogged the fire. On dismounting the following morning our eyes glowed white-rimmed while the rest of our faces were blackened. We looked like the Black and White Minstrels. Thankfully we were not attacked.

10

Egyptian Bin Men and Klefti Wallahs

On one occasion during 1952, a small detachment was sent from Wolseley Barracks, El Ballah to block and protect a desert track leading to El Kantara, the objective being to deter terrorists but it didn't encounter any terrorists. The only Egyptians we saw and searched were shifty looking men on foot, plus others in a beaten up old 2nd World War Dodge platform truck with wooden slatted side panels and no tailboard. The truck was laden with open-topped 40-gallon drums.

The guardsmen searching the peasants on the truck and the contents of the drums quickly covered their mouth and held their nose because although the drums were empty they'd obviously been filled with excreta from crap buckets. Collected from nearby military camps, the contents would end up being dumped in the desert. The air was filled with buzzing black flies and the drums didn't contain stolen fuel as was expected.

I recall similar sewage and pig food trucks kicking up sand while crossing the sandy 'barrack square' in Wolseley Camp followed by a cloud of black flies. The bin men were on their way to empty the 'thunder boxes' housed in three small huts on the edge of the square. What stinking holes those wooden huts were.

When on exercise, grabbing an entrenching tool and digging a hole in the desert sand was a much more hygienic way of 'unloading'. But in camp I'd rather endure lack of privacy while sitting on a pole over a lime filled dugout than sit in these foul fly-infested places. At least the pits could be drenched in paraffin and the contents burnt. But what struck me was the way the Egyptian bin crew delved into drums containing waste food from the messes and stuffed it into their mouths between emptying the crap buckets. Awful!

Looking at the children near the oasis I felt that they'd have a very uncertain future, probably ending up as mature fellahin, living in a small village and sleeping in mud huts as their ancestors had done for centuries. They could look forward to a life of hard work scratching out an existence as a landless peasant farm worker or perhaps a more leisurely life tending goats. But for many, learning the skills of a crafty slick klefti wallah would be the preferred option, followed closely by migration to cities away from toiling in the scorching desert.

Readers who'd served in Egypt will recall that petty thieving was common and will know that one couldn't leave anything unattended for long without it attracting the attention of the silent cunning thief. With my Sten gun under my pillow I used to sleep in a tin hut close to the barbed wire fenced perimeter that the night guard patrolled. At the time I didn't realise that the cheaply produced Sten was not to be trusted due to its habit of firing itself.

But I lacked confidence in the alertness or otherwise of those tasked with patrolling the perimeter. Their orders were to prevent intruders gaining access to the camp and to check the wire for holes and gaps. But I suspected that their main concern would be getting back to the guard-room ASAP, supping a mug of tea and getting their head down. So inevitably quite a lot of kit went missing overnight from camps throughout the Canal Zone.

Organised gangs of cable cutters were a major problem. They planned and executed thieving on a large scale. Hidden from view in the starkness of the desert behind or beneath whatever cover was available, they'd wait until the cable cutting patrols in their well armed jeeps passed and then promptly dig up long lengths of copper communications cable alongside the Treaty Road. A very profitable operation for them.

Worse still was the amount of armaments and ammunition stolen nightly from the huge ammunition dump at Abu Sultan. While posted there the 1st Battalion formed part of the contingent guarding the dump. There it joined the RMP, RAF Police and other dog handlers deployed with their tracker dogs, barker dogs and I suspect killer dogs, searchlight operators and others. But our combined efforts didn't deter the organised Klefti Wallah Mafia.

Coldstreamer John Newton later wrote *'I remember guarding an old dilapidated ammunition dump miles and miles out in the desert. It supposedly had a minefield all the way round it and every so often there was an old wooden tower that one or two guys would sit and talk on the radio to control.*

We guarded it over Christmas 1952 and I remember well opening a can of sardines for my Christmas dinner. We guarded the place 2 days on and 1 day off for about 3 months. Other than reading a good book there wasn't a lot to do and the Bookmobile didn't come around either. It got so cold at nights sleeping in those flimsy tents.'

I feel sure that many readers will have heard about the infamous Egyptian klefti wallahs.

11

Plague of flies

The Plague of Flies was the fourth calamity that according to the biblical Book of Exodus was inflicted upon Egypt to persuade the Pharoah to release the ill-treated Israelites from slavery.

During the plague dog flies were a nasty pestilence. Swarms of blood-sucking flies menaced people and animals. They bit people and even attached themselves to their eyelids and their bites left people swollen and disfigured. The dog flies laid their eggs in various places, such as fermenting vegetation, manure, and garbage. The eggs produced maggots that destroyed the land and the mature dog flies were a very nasty pestilence.

Today, the Blandford Fly is a species of black fly that behaves in a similar way. It breeds beside the River Stour flowing through Blandford Forum close to my home. It attacks locals causing itching and pain leaving them with sore swollen arms, faces and limbs and nasty scars.

Those who served in the Canal Zone will know just how awful the ever-present huge black flies were. Some servicemen and women were bitten by what appeared to be horse flies, possibly descendants of the ancient dog flies. When in camp the latrines would be a favourite scavenging location as were the bin men's trucks as I've indicated above. No matter how deeply into the desert you went swarms of the huge flies were sure to appear as soon as you stopped. There they would pester you seeking out your food and buzzing around forever.

The dreaded mosquitoes

The mosquito parasite requires several days to develop although it still requires blood meals at intervals of 2 to 5 days. By killing them with insecticides before maturation less individuals are infected. I think RAF planes sprayed DDT here and there endeavouring to control the pests but they always posed a menace to any ill prepared servicemen and women.

Sucking Blood - Artist: Poppy Henley

Nearly everyone is sensitive to mosquito bites. We were bitten either at dusk or at dawn when mosquitoes were most active. While male mosquitoes are harmless, feeding only on nectar and water, the females of the species seek out blood. The female mosquito finds her victim by detecting a mix of body odour and sweat, carbon dioxide in exhaled breath, body temperature and movement.

When she finds a suitable meal, she lands on exposed skin in order to drink blood for the nutrients they need to develop eggs. She stabs two tubes into the skin, one to inject saliva containing an anti-coagulant that prevents blood clotting and the other to suck the victim's blood into their bodies. Living in a hot humid climate like Egypt put us at a greater risk because mosquitoes were attracted to our hot bodies.

Mosquito bites transmit serious diseases such as malaria, but recently they've infected thousands in Africa, South America, Florida and South East Asia with the dreadful Zika Virus.

Although we could hear the hum of the mosquito's buzzing wings in flight, they were so crafty that you often didn't realise they'd landed on you at the time. But you knew that you'd been bitten when within 48 hours of the bite soft bumps appeared on your skin that became pink and itchy. We'd normally apply a drop of calamine lotion to ease the discomfort but our Medical Officer had to look after guardsmen that were suffering from lesions, fever, swelling in the throat and breathing problems that required urgent medical attention. Gentian Violet lotion was sometimes prescribed but the famous 'No.9 pills that cure all ills' weren't prescribed for these conditions.

Mosquitoes require standing or stagnant water to breed and as we were based close to the filthy Sweet Water Canal[1] and its adjacent puddles and ponds we had to be careful while on night guard and patrols. Otherwise we tried to avoid water, especially at dusk and dawn when mosquitoes were most active. We wore long-sleeved shirts and long trousers after dusk and at night we slept under a net draped from the roof. The net provided some protection against mosquitoes, flies and other insects and the diseases they carried, but to be effective the mesh had to be fine enough to exclude such insects. Keeping the pests out seemed to reduce airflow and trap our body heat, making us feel really hot and restless. We knew it was possible to increase effectiveness of the net by treating it with a mosquito repellent but we didn't have any!

Somehow the little sods managed to bite us, even though we regularly checked the nets for holes or gaps large enough to allow insects to enter. It was important to fix the net properly because mosquitoes were able to squeeze through insecure nets and as an insect can bite a person through an untreated net, we had to ensure that the net didn't contact our skin. Besides that we didn't want a black scorpion or other creepy crawlies to join us in our bed.

Nowadays long lasting insectide impregnated nets can reduce the number of bites by infected mosquitoes but that's a long time after our ongoing battle with the pests.

---

1. The Sweet Water Canal travels east to west from Lake Timsah to Port Said. Thousands of labourers dug the canal that was designed to provide fresh water for workers building the Suez Canal. For those serving in the Canal Zone during the 1950s the canal was no longer clean but simply an open sewer. It was a place where the dead bodies of tortured civilians and troops could readily be dumped.

12

The celebration of Ramadan

Ramadan in the Canal Zone

Millions of British Muslims celebrate Ramadan for a month annually from sunset on a given day. But for those serving in the Canal Zone during 1952 and 1953 the dates for Ramadan were 23 May-22 June for 1952 and 13 May-12 June for 1953

I must admit that while serving in El Ballah and elsewhere I knew virtually nothing about Ramadan. All I'd heard were humorously indecent tales circulated by our old soldiers describing the local Egyptians' sexual activities. They insisted that Ramadan was a time when the local male Fellahin actively pursued young boys because the women sought to limit sexual urges by banning rampant men from their sleeping quarters. Another story doing the rounds told of frequent visits by Arabs to a hotel in French Square, Ismailia throughout Ramadan. The purpose being to seek favours from 'Peg leg', a legendary French one-legged prostitute. She could be relied upon to keep her mouth shut about her sexual partners provided the price was right, although clients using her services rendered their fast void.

In truth, I must say that while in Wolseley Camp I neither saw evidence of 'Salat', praying five times daily while facing the direction of Mecca, nor the practice of ablution, that is, washing of the body before the prayers. But then I didn't expect to, as the only Arabs I observed were the dhobi wallahs busy all day and night dealing with piles of dirty washing and khaki drill laundry. The nearest they got to washing was spraying starchy liquid between their front teeth onto the fabric but necessarily drinking plenty of water as they worked wielding very heavy steaming hot irons. The visiting sanitary bin men looked pretty filthy as they tipped the contents of thunder boxes into old topless 40-gallon drums and explored the contents of our mess room and cookhouse bins containing kitchen refuse and scraps to be fed to pigs. They seemed to be in an awful hurry, so maybe they weren't truly devoted Muslims. Or perhaps they continued to work during Ramadan because the prophet Muhammed had said that *'it's important to keep a balance between worship and work'*.

The spirit of Ramadan is one of goodwill and a commitment to improving the lives of other people but I'm pretty sure all previously employed locals that had withdrawn labour were now intent on doing all they could to make our lives a misery. Extremists were attempting to overthrow the Government by stirring up trouble and anti-British feeling was running high.

As a result, British troops patrolling the Suez Canal Zone came under attack from rebel gunmen. Ray Applin, my ex. 3rd Battalion The Parachute Regiment pal confirmed this saying that his regiment while on duty in Ismailia had come under automatic fire several times, especially during Ramadan.

Factual background of Ramadan

Islam started in what is now known as Saudi Arabia. Ramadan is derived from Arabic words meaning scorching heat or dryness. The celebration of Ramadan begins when the new moon is sighted in the sky. It's a period of 30 holy days devoted to prayer and recitation of the Qur'an (Koran) throughout the ninth month of the Muslim year. The start time is very important as the month is blessed and marks the commencement of strict fasting from sunrise to sunset.

Ramadan is considered important because the Koran giving guidance for mankind and outlining the difference between right and wrong is said to have been revealed to the Prophet Muhammad during *'The night of power'* near the end of the month. Muslims believe that to pray on this special night is better than 1000 months of day-to-day worship. Believers recite as much of the Koran as they can during Ramadan, a period when the Messenger of Allah said that the gates of Heaven (Paradise) are opened and the gates of Hell closed and devils put in chains there.

Moderate Muslims believe that their good actions bring a greater reward during this month than at any other time of year because Allah has blessed the month. They also believe that it's easier to do good in this month because the devils have been chained in Hell and so can neither deceive nor tempt believers. Muslims also try to give up bad habits believing that this is one way that devils are chained up. But nevertheless evil thoughts and deeds prompted by Satan lurk within them and this compels them to attempt to give up sinful behaviour.

While Muslims fast during other times of the year, for every able-bodied Muslim, Ramadan is the only time when fasting is obligatory during the entire month. It also brings to mind the fate of the poor who seldom get enough to eat. Ramadan is intended to enhance self-control by abstaining from food and drink thereby avoiding gluttony, a deadly sin; so it's an ideal time to lower one's body mass index! What is the point of fasting if after sunset one makes up for all that has been missed during the daytime? For, *'There is nothing more odious to God, than a belly stuffed full of food after a fast'.*

But it is now becoming the norm for 'fasters' to top-up for Ramadan. More food and drink is consumed during Ramadan than is for several other months combined (and suppliers are quick to raise prices accordingly). It is therefore worth reflecting on the primary objective of fasting, which is to experience hunger and to minimise slothfulness (idly sleeping), control sex drive, avoid evil thoughts and deeds and manage their use of available time. All in the interests of self-purification.

Throughout Ramadan the tongue must be restrained from cursing, backbiting, gossiping or speaking obscene words. Eyes must not look at prohibited things. Hands must not touch another's property. Feet mustn't enter sinful places and ears mustn't listen to idle talk. By complying with these instructions every part of the body observes the fast.

A big festival called 'Eid-ul-Fitr' marks the end of the fast. It is the Festival of the Breaking of the Fast. This is when Muslims dress in their finest clothes, give gifts and spend time with their friends and family. Money must be donated to charity to help poor people buy decent clothes and nourishing food so they too can celebrate. Each member of a family that can afford it is under divine obligation to provide a meal or its monetary equivalent to at least one person in need. So as giving during Ramadan is believed to result in greater reward for the giver larger donations than normal are made.

Eid-ul-Fitr is a time of reverence when Muslims praise Allah (God) and pray for forgiveness for sins they have committed. It's a time for making amends. But possibly the greatest thing a Muslim can do is to commit to the Hajj, the pilgrimage to Mecca that each Muslim must make at least once in their lifetime.

13

The Transport Platoon

In Egypt I continued as MT Clerk in the Transport Office with Sgt George Clack continuing as Transport Sgt. While based in Tel-el-Kebir he took the opportunity of making good any deficiencies by raiding the many stores warehouses there. I remember our drivers tearing around the camp driving old Dodge trucks and remnants from the desert warfare of earlier years. The most significant recollection I have is of Trucks 3 ton CL Cargo being used as refuse collection vehicles laden with old 40-gallon oil drums with the lid removed.

Move to El Ballah

We weren't based in Tel-el-Kebir for long and in late February moved to Wolseley Barracks, El Ballah with George still the main man of the Transport Platoon. There he supervised a large unit with about 80 vehicles including Support Company carriers, trailers etc. and something like 60 NCOs and men.

Transport Platoon El Ballah Egypt 1952

I was put on an L/Cpl's Drill Course, came top of the Cadre and was promoted on 14 March 1952. Being a young 'erk' I dreaded the need to give orders to the older time-expired guardsmen who'd served throughout the 2nd World War and later in Haifa, Palestine and Tripoli. Although personally well disciplined these blokes didn't take kindly to enforced retention and tended to do only what they wished to. Hence, whenever possible I left the detailing to George as he could handle old guardsmen like Smith JB the stutterer and Smurthwaite a real tough old soldier.

George wearing his fez and shorts outside the Transport Office

On 25 July 1952 I attended another drill course for promotion to Lance Sergeant and was appointed George's assistant. The photograph taken in the Nissan Hut that served as the Transport Office and Stores shows me working on the AFG3654 Petrol Oil & Lubricants (POL) Account for George to check and approve.

Author then a L/Sgt working on POL Account

I was lucky enough to be sent on a MT Accounting Course held at the REME MT School, Bordon, Hants. So I was dropped off at the Fayid Transit Camp to await a flight to UK. I flew in an Airwork Dakota aircraft that needed to land and refuel at RAF El Adem Airfield near Tobruk Libya, Malta (where we spent the night), Nice and finally Blackbushe Airport near Farnborough.

I did well on the course than ran from 22 September to 4 October 1952, was awarded a Grade 'A' (outstanding) pass and flown back to Fayid in a RAF Hermes. But not before a brief stay in Goodge Street Transit Centre that was once a World War II deep-level air-raid shelter. After the war the Goodge Street shelter beneath the London Underground Station was used as a hostel that could accommodate a large number of servicemen and women and I was one of them.

Soon after I'd returned to El Ballah the current MT Officer was posted elsewhere and replaced by Lieutenant Simon Gillilan Weber-Brown (SGWB) the incoming Transport Officer (the term 'MTO' being no longer used).

He was immediately promoted to Captain and took over command of the Transport Platoon. I felt that George didn't hit it off with Weber-Brown, who didn't seem to know a bonnet from a rear axle. But they got along and SGWB left all the technical stuff to George and me.

He simply used to float into the office with his boxer dog Winston, sign paperwork and depart, sensibly leaving things to us.

Winston - SGWB's pet Boxer enjoying the shade

Sgt Gosling (who was later ordained as a vicar) supervised the Transport Stores. It was staffed by Gdsm Thompson a Regimental boxer employed there as a storekeeper. L/Sgt Harry Simpson joined them later in order to take over from Sgt Gosling on his demob.

We rescued a kitten that had been found wandering around the vehicle park half-starved and gave it a home in the office.

MT cat occupying the Transport Officer's 'in-tray'

But military rules must be complied with! Permission is required to keep an animal in the camp. So under the pretext that vermin had infiltrated the store I had to march into Commanding Officer's Orders clutching the small black and white kitten named 'Tio'. I needed to obtain permission to keep a pet in barracks. I think this was probably a wind-up as the bloody cat kept scratching and wriggling as I marked time in front of Colonel RC Robin OBE, the Commanding Officer, to make my application, which he granted. The cat spent most of the time in SGWB's in-tray in the Transport Office.

Another Drill Course

I attended another Drill Course on 17 May 1953 and was promoted to Full Sergeant and replaced George as Transport Sergeant. He returned to the UK to take up another appointment at the Guards Depot, Caterham. Without the support and training that George lavished on me I wouldn't have been able to do the job well. I'm truly thankful to him for that.

An image of George in Egypt that pops into mind and amuses me no end, is that whenever he got a 'strop on' or if a mini-emergency cropped up or a vehicle was needed in a hurry; he would grab his Service Dress cap, plonk it onto the back of his head and go rushing out of the Transport Office. Then he would stomp off across the parking area, skipping and hopping so as to get to his objective soonest. He'd splutter and rave at a driver and later remove his cap and scratch his head after these exertions. It was not until much later that I learned that George had long before been trapped behind a reversing vehicle and suffered a nasty injury to his legs, hence the hopping around.

But we all valued him and respected him greatly and whenever I think of him I recall his devotion to duty and commitment to his work. Within the MT he was an organised man. He knew his stuff and he treasured the Regiment and all that it stands for and did so until his death. George Clack will always be remembered by surviving members of the Transport Platoon as well as those who served with him at different stages throughout his long and successful career.

I was pleased to be able to write and present a tribute to him at his funeral held in Oxford during September 2015 after which I wrote to his widow:

Dear Pam,

From the time you let me know the bad news I felt so low and saddened to learn that I had lost a lifelong friend who'd been good to me when we were young. I was apprehensive about attending the farewell, not because I was afraid to present the tribute but because I couldn't get my head around the reality that you had to grieve and suffer the pain of losing such a good husband, father and grandfather.

But strangely, while I was writing the tribute I felt close to George, almost as if he were looking over my shoulder - just as he used to in Egypt. This made me feel tranquil and my mind filled with fond memories that I shall cherish always.

And when I met you at the event, a cloud lifted and the warmth of the family closeness lifted my spirit. So that I was pleased to do what I could to inform the mourners of what little I knew and felt for George. I feel sure that his Lordship and the other Coldstreamers present really valued what I had to say and I'm certain that those fellows thought a great deal of George, as did I.

I was taken by surprise when the vicar extracted some of the content and used it as the basis for his reading and sermon, but what I wrote I really meant and this seemed to come through to the mourners as the vicar spoke. A number of people commented that the content we agreed captured his character and truly reflected the man that George was.

Sent with fondest thoughts to you all. I'll never forget George and his family.

Sincerely,

Les Walklin

14

More about the incoming Transport Officer

The photograph below taken at Wolseley Camp, El Ballah during 1953 shows the Transport Officer, Captain (later Major) Simon Gillilan Weber-Brown (SGWB) with the author, then Transport Sergeant of the 1st Battalion. We remained lifelong friends until he died peacefully on 3rd March 2014 aged 84, a true Coldstreamer.

Transport Officer with Transport Sergeant

SGWB like many other gentlemen serving with the Guards was educated at Eton College. He certainly fitted the descriptor *'A gentleman first and a soldier afterwards.'*

Whenever I think of our Etonian gentlemen I recall the Duke of Wellington's favourite solution of the Waterloo riddle *'The Battle of Waterloo was won on the playing-fields of Eton.'*

His fellow officers such as Lieutenant the Hon SWF Crossley (the third Baron Somerleyton), exemplified his social class. This officer commanded the Anti-tank Platoon and frequently visited the Transport Office, officially seeking REME help but content to stay and chat for a while. In his eulogy many years later Major Weber-Brown stated: *'He was born into privilege and had grandeur thrust upon him, but he was never stuck up. He was a decent honourable man and a splendid English gentleman. And looking into the sea of faces I don't mind betting there are many people who see him the same way as I do.'*

Mr Simon Gillilan Weber-Brown at Eton College

The photograph shows SGWB dressed in the traditional uniform of black tailcoat and waistcoat, white tie and pinstriped trousers holding his top hat.

The Duke of Wellington once declared: *'The British army is what it is, because it is officered by gentlemen; men who would scorn to do a dishonourable thing and who have something more at stake before the world than a reputation for military smartness.'*

I count myself lucky to have had the opportunity of serving with gentlemen that were undoubtedly collectively the best of the best.

On one occasion SGWB chastised me when I answered a telephone call from Capt E Fitzroy, a Platoon Commander of No 2 Company. 'You don't say "Sir", you say, "Good morning Lord Edward"'.

I first met SGWB when he flew into Fayid Airfield as a pink-cheeked and freckled sandy-haired young Lieutenant. I picked him up in a 1 ton Morris Commercial truck and dropped him off at the Officers Mess in Wolseley Camp. He was immediately promoted Captain and took over as Transport Officer from Captain FWR Fisher who'd been educated at Winchester and whom I'd worked with for about two years.

A relevant extract from SGWB's Obituary published in The Guards Magazine Journal of the Household Division states: *'Much to everyone's surprise he was made the Motorised Transport Officer and attended a course at Bordon. The Chief Instructor wrote, "Mr. Weber-Brown must overcome his aversion to putting on overalls". With the help of Sergeant Walklin the Battalion Transport ran perfectly and they became firm friends for evermore. Sergeant Walklin attended his funeral at Knossington on the 19th March along with many old Coldstreamers.'*

On the vehicle park

Each day after breakfast SGWB would sit down at his desk in the Transport Office and look through the paperwork in his 'In Tray' having first removed 'Tio' the black and white office cat from its favourite snoozing position. Most of the paperwork he would immediately shove in my direction.

Easing himself upright he'd say, 'Right, Sgt Walklin let's inspect the area.'

'Get the sand swept smooth in front of the office. There are footprints everywhere.'

On to the vehicle park we'd go and along the row of vehicles not currently in use.

'Why isn't that truck in use?'

Thinking that it would be a complete waste of breath explaining the defect I would say, 'It's off-the-road, Sir. Awaiting REME attention.' etc. etc.

Being fair skinned he didn't spend too much time in the sun. This pleased me immensely because it reduced the risk of him specifying some ridiculous 'bullshit' tasks for the men to undertake.

Overalls will be worn

To wind-up SGWB I suggested that he be seen wearing overalls whenever we carried out vehicle inspections. I added that this would enhance his credibility among the platoon. Believe it or not he agreed and within a few days he drove up in a Land Rover and got out suitably attired. I was amazed! There was he wearing smartly-tailored starched and pressed snowy white overalls, white cotton gloves, his cap and shiny black shoes. Immaculately turned out as usual thanks to the efforts of his soldier servant.

Intent on demonstrating his knowledge of transport operations and maintenance and control of things we set off to check the servicing tasks alloted to drivers. I realised that SGWB had not an inkling of what was under the bonnet of a vehicle let alone any technical knowledge of military vehicles. To him such things would remain a mystery. He showed little interest in things mechanical and clearly didn't wish to change his ways.

Discipline

SGWB was a fair disciplinarian and dead keen on proper behaviour and personal turnout. So he was delighted when checking on routine work to be carried out on our Karrier Recovery truck a guardsman driver was caught out stating a falsehood. The driver concerned who'd joined the Regiment at Caterham the same week as me had been ordered to remove the roadwheels, split the rims and repaint them with red-oxide paint. But sadly for him, SGWB spotting a blob of red paint on the nearside front tyre said, 'What's that on the tyre?'

'Have you completed the work you were detailed to do, driver?'

'Yes, Sergeant.'

'Right, well strip the wheel down again and we'll see.'

'I might as well tell you, I haven't done the work.'

'Corporal Smith, march him to the Guardroom. Put him in close arrest, "Stating a falsehood to the Transport Sergeant".'

Next day on Company Orders extra drills were awarded as punishment for lying.

The men didn't give us a lot of trouble but sometimes it was necessary to act promptly in order to maintain discipline. On one occasion Gdsm. 'X', a nervous driver, reported to the Office. He saluted SGWB and I asked him, 'Where's your weapon?'

He blurted out, 'Two corporals seized my truck and weapon at Abu Sueir RAF Camp. I got a lift back here.'

'Right, stop shaking and calm down. Go away and write a full account of what happened. Come back when you've done so and give it to me.'

I then telephoned the Regimental Provost Sergeant in the Guardroom and instructed him to put both L/Cpls in close arrest on their return to camp. This he did.

Next day charged with the offences they were marched into Commanding Officers Orders. RSM bawls, 'Two Lance Corporals shun. March in. Left, right, left... Mark time. Halt.'

Evidence of arrest was given.

'Fall-in. Two Guardsmen march out. Left, right, left....'

Being unable to resist the lure of spending time with two WRAFs resulted in them both paying the penalty. They were busted.

Because we were heavily committed with technical transport-related matters we were joined by L/Sgt Bennett from No. 2 Company. Being a strict discipinarian he was tasked with maintaining day-to-day discipline for our large platoon and ensuring that barrack rooms and kit was up to standard. I was relieved to hand over to him this aspect of my overall role.

Driving matters

I didn't rate SGWB's driving skills. When driving he seemed not to know which gear the vehicle was in and only changed gear as an after-thought. (Years later when he worked in the City he telephoned me saying, 'Walklin, I have a Bentley!' I wondered how he would manage to park the monster in London unless he had brushed up his driving style).

SGWB left much of the driving to me whenever we travelled together. He would sometimes say, 'Sgt Walklin drive me somewhere.'

'Where, Sir?'

'Oh, anywhere. Drive me to the Officer's Mess and I'll pick up a flask of cold orange juice. Then we'll go to Ismailia and buy some humbugs.'

or

'Take me to El Hamada for some duck shooting! You can beat for me and flush them out.'

I had no idea what was involved and reluctantly asked, 'How on earth do I do that?'

'You'll be out in the open working with others as a team flushing the birds from cover toward our guns. You'll have a stick to poke into every bit of cover where the birds will be hiding. Just whack the bushes with the stick and they'll fly off. Other men will wave coloured flags. That'll make the birds fly higher. It's more sporting. Gives them more of a chance to get away and is a challenge for us to hit them too. You'll see some lovely labradors and spaniels there.'

'Well I hope you're a better shot than you are a driver! I'd hate to get buckshot in my backside.'

I was saddened when SGWB left Egypt to spend two years as an ADC to Field Marshal Viscount William Slim KG GCB GCMG GCVO GBE DSO MC KStJ, the Governor-General of Australia where, *'he was in his element telling visiting Kings, Queens and Prime Ministers what to do. He maintained that the more important people were, the easier they were to deal with, especially HM The Queen and Prince Philip.'* But he was without doubt the perfect choice for the ADC role.

A temporary Transport Officer in the form of a young officer replaced SGWB. The officer, Lieutenant Peter Egerton-Warburton promptly left everything for me to do. But he was a really fun guy and the Transport Office staff had a lot of laughs during his attachment.

15

Vehicle types

A few of the vehicle types the 1st Battalion had on strength while in the Canal Zone are shown below. The RAF, RASC, RAOC, REME and Royal Engineers obviously operated a much wider range including specialised vehicles whereas an infantry battalion was somewhat limited and had to make do with what was on offer at the time.

The Humber 'Box' Heavy Utility Car 4x4 FWD

Before enlisting I was a commercial vehicle apprentice to The Rootes Group, owner of formerly independent car companies including Hillman, Humber, Sunbeam-Talbot, Singer and also Commer and Karrier trucks. Being devoted to Rootes' products and working on them for four years I felt I knew every nut and bolt on the Commer/Karrier trucks and particularly their sturdy Humber 6 cylinder side valve engine.

When WW2 came Humber Snipe and Super Snipe cars were produced for use as staff cars. A prominent user of the Humber Snipe being 1st Viscount Field Marshal Bernard Montgomery of Alamein who relied on one during campaigns in North Africa and Europe.

Humber Snipe staff car

Source: http://panzerserra.blogspot.co.uk

Also used was the steel bodied Humber 'Box' derived from the Super Snipe and designed specially for the Army as a Heavy Utility 4 x 4 four-wheel drive. Some had a steel roof while others had a 'tropical' open top fitted with a folding tilt. It was powered by 4.08-litre six-cylinder petrol engine yielding 85 BHP (the same as the engine fitted to our Karrier Winch recovery truck). It had a strong chassis fitted with a (then) novel independent front suspension.

The Humber was used for utilities, armoured reconnaissance cars operated by the RAF Regiment in the Canal Zone for guarding airfields (I think), FFW Wireless trucks, GS trucks and light field ambulances.

Humber Box a Heavy Utility 4 x 4 four-wheel drive

Source: http://panzerserra.blogspot.com

They proved to be sturdy and reliable and remained in service for many years after the end of World War Two and we were lucky enough to get one. So at El Ballah during 1952 when issued with our Commanding Officer's Humber 'Box' I was delighted and took every opportunity I could to drive it. It really was a rugged and reliable vehicle, so good on cross country work and on soft sand too.

Land Rover Series 1

Our Land Rovers were Series One 80 inch wheelbase models built between 1948 and 1951. They were powered by a 1595cc 50 hp 4 cylinder engine with such a low compression ratio (only 6.8:1), that they would run on almost any grade of petrol. The engine was rather unusual in that it had overhead inlet valves with side valve exhaust. We found that this layout caused them to use a good deal of OMD110 mineral based engine oil. They did about 15 mpg.

Initially the drivers crashed 1st and 2nd gears until they got used to them because the gearbox had syncro-mesh on 3rd and top gear only. But the transmission design came in handy on the soft sand as the Land Rover had a form of permanent four wheel drive with a 2 speed transfer box and high and low range gears. Driving along a hard road, on the overrun, the free wheel would disengage the front axle from manual drive unless the driver locked it.

Land Rover Series 1

The photograph shows an almost deserted parking area (in Tel-el-Kebir I think). An Austin K5 4x4 3 Tonner can be seen in the background with a 3 Ton Austin 4x2 CL Cargo truck parked nearby facing the opposite way. A variety of trailers are parked there. The upturned ones are metal bodied. Not a scenario to be proud of.

At El Ballah and elsewhere a Land Rover and driver was allocated daily to each of the five Company Commanders and the revered Lt-Col (QM) Sidney 'Duff' Cooper MBE; the remainder being used for general duties. A couple of quite heavily laden Land Rovers survived an expedition across the Sinai Desert although some drivers preferred the Jeep. We only had one of those 'go anywhere' super vehicles.

Morris Commercial 15 cwt C4

We were originally issued with a few Morris Commercial 15 cwt GS 4x2 trucks powered by a 3.5 litre 4 cylinder petrol engine.They were designed to carry the heavy personal equipment of an infantry platoon.

Morris Commercial 15 cwt GS 4x2 truck

They were useful for lifting bedding, blanket rolls, big packs, ammo and rations when on active service or exercises. But we used them mainly for any day-to-day jobs that didn't justify the use of 3 tonners. The photograph shows one of the trucks receiving attention from the topless REME L/Cpl outside his work station - not much of a garage! Gdsm Roy Wilson is seen looking on.

Morris Commercial 1 Ton 4x4 truck

After a while we took on strength about a dozen later model 1 Ton Morris Commercial trucks that were 4 wheel drive and much more comfortable to drive.

Ford WOT6 Three-ton GS 4x4 truck

These Ford 3 tonners were produced from 1942 to 1945. They were available in various forms including load carriers, troop carriers, office trucks and ambulances. You name it, they did it.

The Battalion was issued with about 20 Three-ton WOT6 GS 4x4 trucks fitted with a 4-speed gearbox and 2-speed transfer box. They were the main workhorses of the Transport Platoon. We also had one Bedford Office truck and an easy to drive Austin K5, renowned for the screaming noise emanating from its transfer box. These front-line cargo trucks were four-wheel drive. All were forward control with steel bodies, removable frames and canvas tilt.

The Fords were powered by a V8 flat head side valve 3621cc petrol engine rated at 85HP. The trouble with these petrol engines was that they were 'gutless', with drivers complaining that it took one bank of cylinders to cause the other bank to turn over.

The gear lever not being 'ergonomically designed' could make the left shoulder ache as drivers needed to 'row' laden trucks along by constantly changing gear. Fuel consumption therefore was high. They were supposed to do about 8 mpg but ours only managed about 4 mpg. Making me wonder whether or not some of the truck loads of filled jerry cans picked up from the POL Depot changed hands en route back to El Ballah with subsequent fiddling of the work tickets and petrol issues.

Ford WOT6 Three Tonner

We reluctantly tried towing the heavy refrigerated ration trailer behind a Ford, but gave up and opted to use our Karrier K6 recovery truck for the daily journey to collect the unit's rations. What a difference this made. The truck never let us down and the drivers thought the world of it.

The photo taken in Cyprus shows the vehicle displaying the 3rd Infantry Division signs. It was still painted in olive drab. The fellow posing hadn't managed to get his knees brown and looks as if he could do with a good meal.

Our trusty Karrier Ration Wagon

Karrier was established by Clayton & Company in 1907 but the company was taken over by the Rootes Group in 1934 and production moved to Luton. The Karrier K6 truck was introduced in late 1940. The first order for the British Army was for 500 trucks with a timber general service (GS) cargo body. Subsequently 1 625 were fitted with a 4½-ton vertical-spindle winch placed just ahead of the rear axle.

The K6 remained in British service after the Second World War and about 500 had the new style serials (00YY01 - 40YY95) allocated in 1949. Our Karrier Truck 3 Ton CT Cargo 4x4 w/w (with winch) shown in the photograph was numbered 15YY52. The last K6 left British service around 1965.

Karrier Truck 3 Ton CT Cargo 4x4 w/w towing ration trailer

Austin Ambulance K2

The most numerous British ambulance during WW2 was the Austin K2/Y 4x2 Heavy Ambulance. Nick named 'Katie', 13 000 were produced and we had one of them. The body was of simple construction comprising a wooden frame covered with leathercloth. It was well insulated, heated and accommodated four stretchers or eight sitting cases or combinations of both, plus a medical attendant. The body design was the result of much pre-war development work by the Royal Army Medical Corps. It was produced by Mann Egerton, the specialist luxury car body builders.

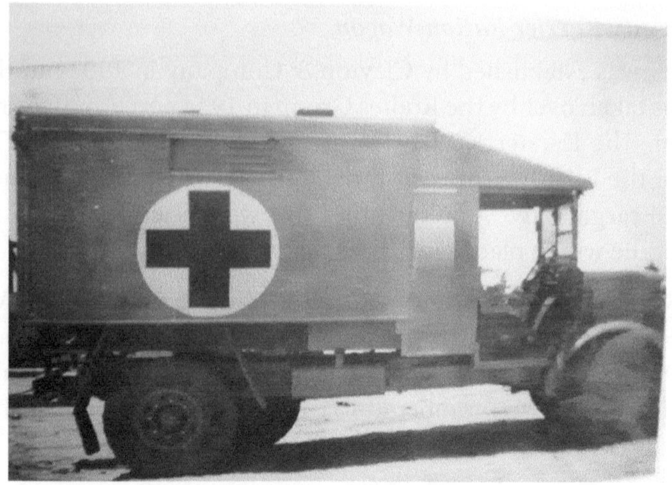

Austin K2/Y 4x2 Heavy Ambulance

Daimler Scout Car - Dingo

I don't have a photograph of our Dingo so a photograph provided compliments of the 12th Lancers is shown below. Ours was seldom used but always available for the Commanding Officer or Intelligence Officer.

Daimler Scout Car

The small 4 wheel drive armoured Daimler Scout Car was intended to be used as a fast reconnaissance vehicle as it was capable of 55mph. It accommodated two soldiers and was fitted with a No 19 wireless set and normally armed with a .303 Bren Gun or .55 Boys Anti Tank Rifle.

Powered by a Daimler 6 cylinder 2.5 litre petrol engine it gave 55 HP, sufficient to cover ground quickly. For some drivers getting the thing moving was a bit of a puzzle because it had pre-selector gears and a fluid flywheel with 5 forward and 5 reverse gears!

I recall selecting forward gear, revving up the engine and then kicking a pedal down and off we went. It could go as fast backward as it could forward.

It was designed by BSA and produced by Daimler whom I thought made a better job of it than the heavy BSA 500cc side valve motor bike that I rode in Egypt.

BSA M20 500cc motorcycle

The bike was produced in large quantities during WW2 and it remained in service throughout the war and after the war during the 1950s. It was heavy and slow with poor ground clearance but it was reliable and easy to maintain. Spares were readily available and seemed to last quite well. It was used by convoy escorts and signals despatch riders and coped well in the harsh desert conditions. We were unlikely to get issued with a Matchless or AJS so we made do with the trusty old girder-forked BSA.

BSA M20 500cc at El Ballah

16

On guard in Egypt

Moascar guard duties 1952-53

A detachment of the 1st Battalion Coldstream Guards was sent to Moascar in order to mount guard and strengthen security there and in nearby Ismailia. The photograph reproduced to the left shows Drum Major Tilley leading the Corps of Drums. There as in UK today, military bands and guard mounting attracts spectators, a few of whom can be seen on the pavement.

Drum Major Tilley leads the Corps of Drums

The photograph on the right shows the Battalion drum and pipe band leading the guard found by No 2 Company.

Corps of Drums leading the guard

The guardsmen are marching with fixed bayonets. They have obviously come some distance because they have changed arms with their polished Lee Enfield 303 Rifle resting on their right shoulder.

The NCO right guide for the guard is L/Sgt 'Benito' Bennett so nicknamed because he had a slightly swarthy colouring and looked a bit like an Italian. Behind him, with a pace stick under his left arm, is WO2 (Drill Sergeant) Leslie Trimming who'd later be promoted WO1 (RSM). He took others and me on the drill courses we needed to pass in order to qualify for each promotion.

L/Sgt Bennett was a 'dead regimental' NCO, exceptionally keen on maintaining discipline and ensuring that his kit and turnout was always to the very highest standard. He demanded that the same degree of excellence should apply to the guardsmen whom he supervised.

Guard mounting in Moascar

Benito and me first met in the Receiving Room at the Guards Depot when joining the Regiment as recruits. We remained together throughout the six months training before being posted to the 1st Battalion where we maintained a close friendship until I left the Regiment.

Benito 'signed on' for further service but was killed some years later in a military road traffic accident whilst returning to Windsor in a truck. So sad.

Abu Sultan deployment

In December 1952 a large detachment was sent to Abu Sultan Base Ammunition Depot where it was to stop the Egyptians from stealing materiel. It was rumoured that each night the Egyptians were stealing 6 tons of ammunition. My role as Transport Sergeant was to provide and maintain transport to ferry the patrols here and there and carry out other support duties.

The considerable drop in temperature at night caused havoc initially, as most of our trucks were 3 Ton Ford WOT 6 V8 petrol-engined with the ignition distributor located just behind the radiator. This resulted in dampened ignition leads and non-starting problems. So to overcome the problem I ordered drivers to start up and run the engines every two hours. This kept the ignition system dry. What would we have given for vehicles fitted with diesel engines?

There were barker dog, tracker dog and probably killer dog patrols mounted by professional dog handlers and it was necessary for us to deploy observers by day. But at night under the cover of darkness hundreds of men were required to guard and patrol the miles of mined perimeter wire. At dusk the Transport Platoon role was to ensure that the observers and patrols were conveyed to variable positions without being spotted by any would-be thieves. Fortunately no casualties were sustained and no one was blown to pieces by unmarked mines. We later heard that no ammunition had been stolen on our watch.

17

Double trouble

During October and November 1952 the 1st Battalion took part in Brigade and Divisional Exercises in the south and if my memory serves me rightly I recall getting a call from the Commanding Officer who was in the Bedford Office Truck somewhere in the desert. He gave me a map reference and said, *'Sgt Walklin send me a chair right away.'*

It was late and not wishing to drag a driver from his pit I asked L/Sgt Harry Simpson, my storekeeper, to grab his Sten gun and a chair. We somehow crammed into our Daimler Scout Car with Harry perched on the chair in the turret and sped off into the desert. We came across a narrow sandy track close to a river near the map reference and spotted lights.

'That's it. Let's go along the track.'

Not a good idea. We were heading towards an Egyptian army encampment in the desert. I was driving when Harry screamed out, 'Quick, turn around.'

I attempted to do a quick multi-point turn but got bogged down almost to the belly plates. The resulting wheel spin caused the belly plate to almost touch the sandy surface. We were stuck just like a beetle on its back. We climbed down and found that I could just get my hand between the plate and the soft sand. So we scrabbled away with our bare hands digging away like rabbits to clear sand from the front and rear of each wheel. Then we quickly got back in. I revved flat out and kicked the pedal down and thankfully got moving amid a cloud of dense blue smoke. We were ecstatic to have got away with it. We'd escaped before the Egyptians realised what was happening. But I didn't explain the reason for delay to the Commanding Officer.

It seems that Harry and I tempted Providence on more than one occasion when an officer ordered a Land Rover to transport him from El

Ballah to Ismailia where he was to dine with very senior Staff Officers. With Harry as my escort we drove to the Officers' Mess and picked up the officer, drove to the destination without trouble and set him down. He told us to lose ourselves and return at 'X' hours. And lose ourselves we certainly did.

On the way to the return pick-up point we unintentionally drove into an Egyptian Army Barracks passing a sentry who was leaning against a sentry box smoking.

'Oh Gawd! Got your Sten, Harry?'

'No, its in pieces. I locked it up under my seat.'

'Well f---ing well get it sorted.'

While Harry struggled to extricate the weapon from beneath his seat, I drove flat out around the barracks and out of the gate with Egyptians screaming and rushing about like lunatics.

Return to El Ballah

Toward the end of the month having fulfilled the commitment the 1st Battalion returned to El Ballah and the boredom of day-to-day duties. There the Battalion eagerly awaited the order to return to the United Kingdom. The 'time-expired' old soldiers were retained in Egypt for several months after their release date in 1952 due to the shortage of transport home. They were quite difficult to handle especially for a young NCO such as me. They were 'bolo' and couldn't be blamed for appearing to occasionally have a 'couldn't-care-less' attitude. But nevertheless when necessary they remained highly disciplined men and we younger soldiers learned a lot from them.

The Transport Platoon prepared vehicles for several expeditions across the Sinai desert. The objective of one such expedition being to visit St. Catherine's Monastery, built on the site of the Burning Bush as seen by Moses. On return the drivers were debriefed and one reported that the expedition leader Major DFD 'Dead Ground' Noel, Officer Commanding No 2 Company, reportedly a keen botanist, seemed intent only to comb the desert for rare plant life. All returned safely.

18

HANGING THE BRICK - A COLDSTREAM GUARDS REGIMENTAL CUSTOM

Historical background

Battle of Waterloo and Hougoumont Farm 18 June 1815

At the Battle of Waterloo in June 1815 the 2nd Bn Scots Guards was positioned on the ridge just behind Hougoumont Farm, while the light companies of two battalions (2nd Coldstream Guards and 2nd Scots Guards) under the command of Lieutenant-Colonel James Macdonnell garrisoned the Farm; a place on the right flank of the British and Allied army that would be a key position during the battle.

The four Light Companies of the two Guards regiments and Third Guards were tasked with defending the farmhouse of Hougoumont, which the Duke of Wellington later described as the key to the battle. The objective being to provide flanking fire to support Wellington's troops if Napoleon's forces advanced as was expected. If Hougoumont had been lost, Wellington's flank would have been turned and the outcome of the battle may have been very different.

The night before the battle guardsmen manning the walls prepared barricades and defences. Using bayonets, they dug loopholes in the 8 ft. high garden wall large enough to poke their muskets through and fire at the enemy. Fire-steps were also built enabling the defenders to fire over the wall. Guardsmen could then rain down continuous fire, enabled by proficient loaders passing reloaded weapons up to those on the fire step. If the French were to progress it would be 'over their dead bodies!'

On 18 June 1815 Napoleon launched assault after assault during a furious attack by 30 000 blue-coated French infantry to capture this key position. The frantic battle raged from 11am to 8pm during which a French Sous Lieutenant wielding an axe broke through the wooden gates and a group of French soldiers rushed into the farm. But as the

French forced the gates red-coated guardsmen kept them at bay. Sergeant Graham VC (then a corporal) of the Coldstream Guards, along with Lieutenant-Colonel Macdonnell of the Third Guards managed to ram the gates shut trapping the French inside, all of whom were killed except for a drummer boy, thereby saving Hougoumont from capture.

Flagstones, farm carts and debris were then piled against the closed gates. Desperate close-quarters fighting, man to man with bayonets and swords was ruthless. But despite the weight of men and arms thrown at them for hours on end the defenders held their ground. The four light companies held firm until reinforcements in the form of the 2nd Bn Coldstream Guards arrived soon after and quickly repulsed the French attack.

Elsewhere as night began to fall, Bonaparte made a final assault throwing his fearsome Imperial Guard at Wellington's death-defying redcoat lines. But this time they'd met their match. Volleys of musket fire from the right flank cut down many of the French and Wellington set his own Guards upon them with a cry of *'Up and at 'em'*. With gallantry unsurpassed, the front line of guardsmen raced forward attacking with fixed bayonets in a heroic charge, screaming like demons. Astonished by this bravery the Imperial Guard panicked shouting *'Sauve qui peut'* (every man for himself) and fled as fast as their legs would carry them. Seeing this Wellington ordered, *'Forward and complete your victory'* which they did. Bonaparte left the battlefield his dreams of world domination in tatters.

But Wellington admitted that it was *'a desperate action'* and the outcome *'a damned close thing'*. He praised his soldiers saying *'the Army never upon any occasion conducted itself better.'*

Sadly though, the butcher's bill for the battle was frightful with over 50 000 dead and wounded.

Some years later an English Clergyman left £500 in his will to be given *'to the bravest man in England.'* Wellington was invited to nominate that man and he chose Lieutenant-Colonel James Macdonnell who immediately shared the money with Sergeant James Graham VC.

A historian later wrote: *'Probably the gallantry of the defenders of Hougoumont Farm has never been surpassed on any battlefield.'*

Hanging the Brick

This is a Warrant Officers and Sergeants Mess tradition dating back to 1815 the time of Waterloo. The symbolic brick representing flagstones stacked during defence of Hougoumont Farm entrance is hanged at Christmas time. The origin of 'Hanging the Brick' procedures is uncertain but the ceremony has been re-enacted over many years. The brick is held securely in the unit guardroom the day before it is to be hanged. If the corporals and guardsmen are able to obtain the brick they can ransom it for whatever they want. Consequently it is the duty of all WOs & Sgts Mess members to protect it.

Mess members attired in fancy dress march to the Guardroom and collect the brick. The senior Mess member who is shortly due to leave the army usually carries the brick. Two senior Mess members found the 'escort to the brick'. The Mess then march with the brick around the barracks and head for the Officers' Mess where a drink is provided. The formation then heads back to the WOs & Sgts Mess. There are normally ambushes on route and the brick is defended vigorously.

Once the brick is formally hung above the Mess Bar anyone touching it must buy drinks all round. Junior officers inevitably are targeted, bullied and forced to touch the brick although sometimes even appearing willing to part with their money and buy the beer for all and sundry in the Mess. The brick is hanged above the bar until New Year's Day.

At Xmas 1952 the procedure followed at El Ballah was to appoint three members of the WOs and Sgts Mess to collect the 'brick' from the Guardroom and attach it to the top of a flagstaff. The 'escorts' for the brick were WO2 (Drill Sgt) Leslie Haywood Trimming, Sgt Jim Grindley the Pioneer Sgt who carried the brick suspended from the flagstaff and to his left WO2 (Drill Sgt) Douglas Herbert Glisson. Sgt Marcus Cummings of No 2 Company dressed in a straw skirt made from 'Double Century' strong ale wrappers is the photographer shown in the photograph.

Escort collecting the Brick from Guardroom

RSM and Escort 'Trooping the brick' at El Ballah, Xmas 1952

The 'brick' was duly presented to WO1 (RSM) James 'Tin Head' Cowley DCM who, dressed as The Devil (quite appropriately I thought), trooped the brick around the camp together with the two Drill Sgts as escorts.

Following were Mess Members many of whom wore fancy dress. The object of the 'troop' was to make their way to collect junior officers from the comfort of the Officers' Mess.

The gentlemen were 'invited' to join the rear of the throng. Along the route to hang the brick above the Mess bar 'ambushes' were staged and projectiles thrown at the disorderly marchers.

As described above, once hung anyone accidentally touching the brick, being lifted up forcibly, thrown at the brick or otherwise making contact would be forced to buy drinks all round. Naturally, the young officers became prime targets and they were bullied into touching the brick, hence the reason for their 'invites'.

Another victim, treated differently was a really little fellow, Sgt 'Stitch' the Master Tailor, who was lifted up by Sgt 'Legs' McKenna and attached to the large Mess fan above. The fan was then set to revolve!

The ceremony of 'Hanging the Brick' included the reading of 'The Scroll' - see opposite.

Hanging the Brick

Pray silence all ye Coldstreamers gathered here in this hallowed place. We, the members of this distinguished Company are assembled to commemorate the deed of a most courageous gentleman. For those who may not be familiar with the origins of this tradition, I shall render forthwith the relevant details.

The Brick you see before you is an original Brick taken from Hougoumont Farm in the year 1815 AD at the Battle of Waterloo. It was at this farm that Sgt James Graham of the Coldstream Guards earned the title of the Bravest Man in the British Army by physically holding the gate against a series of determined assaults. This ceremony is performed annually wherever Coldstreamers serve to ensure his deeds are never forgotten.

While the Brick hangs whomsoever may wish to touch it may do so. But will automatically be granted the Privilege of providing all manner of beverages for those assembled herein with which to drink to the gallant Sgt Graham.

I now declare the Brick well and truly hung.

Sgt McKenna was a very tall man and I recall that he was my Platoon Sgt during fieldcraft and weapon training at Pirbright Camp, Surrey and the surrounding training areas and later for Battle Training at Pickering, Yorkshire.

A favourite 'game' played in the Mess was 'Poker Dice' or 21 aces. The six-sided dice, which instead of having up to six pips on each face, have playing cards depicting an Ace, King, Queen, Jack, 10 and 9. Several dice were passed around the players and at Stage One the player throwing the requisite number of aces ordered the drink (any concoction at all including ink, lighter fuel, spirits etc.), the Second Stage required the thrower to pay for the drink and the unfortunate who threw the 21st ace had to drink it regardless of the consequences.

Further details can be seen on *www.ShinyCapstar.com* and You Tube.

19

Sensory deprivation and boredom

Sensory deprivation, where a person is starved of sensory inputs, leads to boredom and inability to concentrate effectively. Information is picked up by the five senses that link our central nervous system with the environment and allow us to react accordingly. If we detect no stimuli then we will rapidly drop off to sleep or become seriously depressed. In fact sensory deprivation can be used as a form of torture. We need our senses to be activated in order to function.

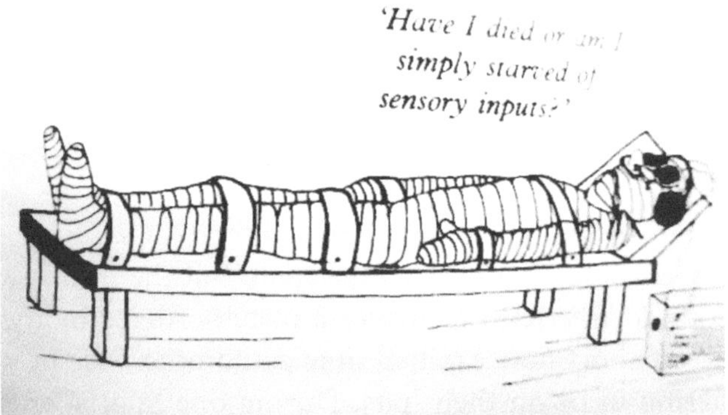

Sensory deprivation experimental set-up

In the 1950s, sensory deprivation experiments were conducted to determine the effects of restricted environmental stimulation on mental and physical functions. For 24 hours a day students were confined to a bed in cramped cubicles with their vision and hearing blocked by various means, such as opaque goggles and U-shaped pillows around their heads. The students' physical and psychological functions quickly deteriorated under these harsh conditions. While the Coldstreamers were not subjected to imposed sensory deprivation, the effects of endless periods of the same boring routine day in day out did affect some of them in a similar way.

How many Canal Zoners succumbed to losing attention or worse still falling asleep while on night guard with little to see or hear throughout the long night?

On returning to the UK, one night when patrolling the Bank of England posts as Sergeant of the Bank Piquet, I found a guardsman fast asleep comfortably seated on a dustbin in a quiet carpeted corridor. Either lack of stimuli or sleep deprivation had obviously affected him and he subsequently had to face the unpleasant consequences.

Boredom

In conventional usage, boredom is an emotional or psychological state experienced when an individual is left without anything in particular to do, is not interested in his or her surroundings, or feels that a day or period is dull or tedious. This aptly describes how many servicemen and women felt, stuck in the Canal Zone. For most guardsmen the 18 months at El Ballah was a most boring and frustrating time.

Wolseley Camp was typical of other camps dotted around the Canal Zone; it was unwelcoming, uncomfortable, too hot and plagued with enormous black flies that gave us little peace. The main occupation seemed to be doing little other than stopping the cunning and persistent Egyptian thieves stealing our belongings.

Recreation was limited to swimming in the Suez Canal, a football kickabout or a game of cricket on the sand. But the troops were not at all inclined to form cricket teams for a match ordered by the company commander at short notice, when they could otherwise be sweating it out slumbering in or on their 'pits'. During one 'sports' afternoon the Duty Drummer's bugle sounded Headquarter Company 'fall-in'. Soon a huge motley crowd dressed in shorts or denims and without weapons formed three ranks and the Company Commander Major Richard Culling Carr-Gomm Croix de Guerre called for volunteers to form two teams. Not a soul stepped forward. This so infuriated the cricket-mad major who promptly ordered the Company Sergeant Major to march the unfortunates around the El Ballah Triangle. Good job the terrorists weren't around to shoot them up!

The Major's love of cricket is revisited in a later account.

A few fortunate fellows briefly escaped the boredom. Coldstreamer John Newton played football for the Army team that flew out of Fayid to

Malta to play an Italian team. But the Avro York they were flying in lost an engine as it came in to land in Valetta. This caused the team and 15 other soldiers on board to be stranded in Malta for about three weeks. Lucky buggers.

John played in goal and was the only Coldstreamer in the team but there were two Grenadiers that played inside left and outside left. The rest of the team was made up from other regiments. The Army played the Italian team three times, winning the first two games 3-1 and 5-1 and drawing the third game 3-3. The Army also beat an RAF team in a match played in Deversoir.

Another lucky group travelled south across the Sinai Desert to visit St. Catherine's Monastery built on the site of the Burning Bush seen by Moses. The expeditions could see the Bush (at that time) within the walls of the Monastery. Apparently, Moses was keeping a flock for his father-in-law when an angel of the Lord appeared to him in a flame of fire out of the midst of the bush that was burning but not consumed and God called to Moses from the bush telling him to bring his people out of Egypt. One possible explanation of the phenomenon is that this type of bush (*Dictamnus fraxinella)* gives off an inflammable vapour into the surrounding air - spontaneous combustion?

A few managed to visit Port Said or Ismailia when the political situation permitted and visitors were not likely to be attacked but for the majority a boring life was spent behind barbed wire.

20

EL BALLAH BLUES

El Ballah was originally a signal station located a few miles south of El Kantara on the Suez Canal. There were three old camps there constructed between the Suez Canal and Sweet Water Canal two miles inland. The 1st Battalion Coldstream Guards occupied Wolseley Camp located directly alongside the Treaty Road. Nearby Gordon Camp was the main camp housing Headquarters (HQ) 32nd Guards Brigade, Royal Artillery units and a mix of other attached units and garrison troops together with the garrison church, St. Michael's the Archangel. The third camp, Gothic Camp situated about five miles from the Sweet Water Canal housed the 1st Battalion Bedfordshire & Hertfordshire Regiment.

El Kantara outpost

Nearby El Kantara was a strategically important place, as the main ferry[2] across the northern half of the Suez Canal operated from there. The pumping station, run by Royal Engineers and others, supplied all fresh-water supplies for the Egyptian Garrison in Northern Sinai. Coldstream guardsmen mounted night guards in and around the pumping station.

---

2. A ferry had operated there for centuries and did so while we were there. But a new 70m high, 4000m long and 404m main span x 10m wide road bridge, *The Mubarak Peace Bridge* over the Suez Canal was built by a Japanese Consortium and opened on 9th October 2001.

No 3 Company, 1st Battalion Coldstream Guards was initially detached at El Kantara, while the Support Company Medium Machine Gun (MMG) Platoon covered the track leading into El Kantara and El Ballah from the desert.

El Firdan swing-bridge across the Suez Canal

The bridge shown was replaced after being destroyed during the Arab-Israeli Six day War in 1967. [3]

Like us the Beds & Herts Regiment was often tasked with guarding the El Firdan railway swing bridge across the Suez Canal. The bridge was lifted and lowered manually by local labour operating some kind of hand-winding mechanism. Once the bridge was lowered to close the shipping lane, trains could rattle across and disappear into the far distance heading toward the Sinai Desert.

Regular armed mobile cable cutting patrols were organised in an attempt to stop the Egyptians digging up and stealing telephone cable. But this proved to be a fruitless exercise. Our main occupation seemed to be safeguarding personal kit and unit resources from reaching the hands of cunning and persistent local thieves.

Concerning theft, Coldstreamer John Newton tells of how Sgt Ilsley of

3. On 14th November 2001 a replacement bridge was inaugurated by President Mubarak. The El Firdan Railway Bridge, the longest 'swing bridge' in the world (640m long x 60m high) runs from the west of the Suez Canal to the east into Sinai. It opens to allow ships to pass in the canal and closes during the passage of trains.

the Signal Platoon 'lost' his rifle at El Ballah during 1953. John wrote,

'On the night before the big parade Sgt Ilsley had been cleaning his rifle before supper time and had left the bolt on his bedside locker. One of the funniest things was to see his face the following morning. He'd got up late, quickly shaved and got dressed and should have been on parade at 0800 hours. Reaching behind his mosquito net for his rifle (which was not secure in the armoury) he found that it was missing. He quickly ran over to inform the Regimental Sgt Major of his plight, only to be told to report immediately to the Guardroom. And to be on orders after the parade. Whoever did it only stole the rifle and didn't take the bolt. So those of us living together in the same area knew that the Sergeant would have to go on parade carrying just his bolt!'

Regrettably, John doesn't explain who'd taken the rifle, why they did it and what were the consequences for Sgt Ilsley. So we shall never know the outcome.

Like thousands of other servicemen and women it was really boring spending months doing little or nothing; with little prospect of an early return to UK. Recreation was limited to scrounging a lift on a 3-tonner either to the Suez Canal for a swim or to the local AKC cinema for a film in the evening (if one were lucky). A real treat would be an outing to the Blue Lagoon, Lake Timsah or the Great Bitter Lake if one could fiddle a trip to the 'seaside'.

Our Regimental Sergeant Major, being a religious man, organised a truck on Sundays for the few who opted for a ride to St. Michael's the Archangel to be 'cleansed of all unrighteousness'. I often drove the 3-tonner and would join the congregation rather than just sit outside in the truck. On one occasion the Padre based his sermon on 1 Peter 5:8 *'Stay alert! Watch out for your great enemy, the Devil. He prowls around like a roaring lion, looking for someone to devour.'*

'Yes', I thought, 'I know what you mean', as I related the concept to my recruit training at the Guards Depot. For 'Devil' substitute 'superintending sergeant' and be watchful always trying to avoid his persecuting glare, reprimands and punishments.

Wolseley Camp was typical of other camps dotted around the Canal Zone. Troops loathed mornings, watching the sun creeping above the desert sands knowing that they'd have a parade before breakfast and work in the intense heat afterwards. They'd be glad when the sun had gone down in a blaze of golden red fading quickly to darkness, culminating in total blackness with thousands of stars twinkling, although the sky was sometimes silvered by moonlight. But even so, the unrelenting heat was still quite oppressive until the coldness of the desert night cooled things down.

The desert between Wolseley Camp and the Suez Canal was dead flat and one could often see the white superstructure of troopships sailing to or from the Far East. They appeared to be sailing across the desert and after spending 18 months at El Ballah guardsmen longingly dreamt of the day they'd be aboard a ship sailing back to UK.

For some this eventually happened but sadly, later due to the UK and USA governments' objection to Nasser's closeness to the Soviet Union, they cancelled funding for the Aswan Dam. Nasser responded by nationalising the Suez Canal. So many Canal Zoners would be back again in 1956 within a few months of finally evacuating the Zone.

21

Activities in the Canal Zone

The average guardsman, like many other servicemen and women didn't like hearing the duty drummer's bugle sounding reveille! The desert air was still cold after the night and one shivered first thing after leaving the warmth of the pit.

The routine was to remove the Sten gun from beneath the pillow and move quickly to the nearby open air washroom for a cold water wash and shave. The nearest shower took the form of a Heath Robinson contraption comprising an elevated 40-gallon drum filled with water from which one could get a soaking by pulling a long chain.

But even so it was always pleasing to see the sun creeping above the tinted horizon, silhouetted against dawn's pink and orange glow in the east. But not for the unfortunates who had to drive all day in the oppressive heat.

Driving beside the Sweet Water Canal

The nearby Sweet Water Canal was anything but sweetly fragranced for it was contaminated with parasites and wreaked of the stench of death. When driving on the Treaty Road alongside the canal the smell was putrid. Bloated dead animals could be seen floating along on the slow moving filthy water together with all sorts of rubbish and waste dumped into it. The fellahin probably thought it easier to dispose of agricultural waste and animal corpses in the canal rather than to bury them in the desert for vermin to devour.

To think that the Royal Engineers somehow managed to detox the water is amazing, for to drink this unpurified liquid would certainly be the last drink you'd ever swallow!

But even so, the contaminated waterway was a precious source used by agricultural workers to irrigate their tomato and potato smallholdings. A young lad wielding a stick could be seen keeping a donkey-powered waterwheel going as the poor animal trod an endless circular path. Round and round the donkey would go causing a primitive rotating bucket-filling apparatus to pick up and deliver water to shallow trenches.

Searching the villages

Distant desert sand plains stretched across either side of our vehicles. Followed by our armed escort truck we occasionally drove past a palm-fringed wadi with a cluster of ruined yellow sandstone buildings. Elsewhere we came across a number of whitewashed mud brick houses that could be loosely termed villages. These villages were dotted with dilapidated homes for camel drovers and goatherds sometimes with a few bleating goats or sheep for milk in nearby stone-walled livestock pens.

The 1st Battalion was frequently tasked with searching these compounds for stolen items, as were the Parachute Regiment and other units.

Once within the darkened hovels the disgusting stench of rank body odours, animal urine and stocks of forage gathered for the winter - well past its sell-by date greeted us. Hawk-nosed black-bearded men wearing traditional hooded linen or woollen djellabas reaching down to the ground, with curved knives stuck in their belt lurked inside. And we couldn't see what they might be concealing.

The hoods protect herdsmen from the sun and prevent sand blown by desert winds blasting their faces. They also prevent heat loss during the bitterly cold winter nights experienced in the desolate landscape. Guardsmen learned to carefully check these hoods for weapons etc. because they contained large pockets covering the neck that might be used to conceal offensive items as well as essential provisions needed while crossing in the desert.

The more worldly-wise Arab thieves were active in the black market and an undisclosed number of green coloured jerricans filled with fuel were thought to change hands and a lively trade in rations and other commodities was presumed to take place on a regular basis!

Dotted here and there were peasant's camps with filthy white-walled huts under rusty corrugated iron roofs, no doubt purloined long ago from military stores. Lean dogs were seen either scavenging for something to eat or else lazing in whatever shade they could find, always barking whenever the military were nearby.

22

Driving in the Canal Zone and Sinai Peninsula

The roads were not safe from ambush, so vehicles carrying armed escorts travelled in two's or well guarded convoys. Each day large numbers of trucks and Land Rovers traversed the 120-mile route from Port Said to Port Tewfik and the City of Suez. Driving along the pot-holed metalled Treaty Road was not good but much better than when driving on the open desert roads.

Few if any road signs pointed the way and as no GPS systems or satellite navigation was available at the time finding one's way across little used desert tracks was problematic. So we needed to brush up on our desert navigation skills before departing into the unknown. Furthermore, military signs erected were quickly sabotaged or 'adjusted' to confuse drivers.

Littering the side of roads and tracks were gutted rusting wrecks of abandoned vehicles that had not yet been 'recovered' by Egyptian scrap dealers. The desert winds shrieked creating swirling dust clouds across the barren land and balls of camel thorn brush tumbled across the road causing drivers to awaken from their semi-dozing driving mode.

Sometimes a humming radio would squawk, screech or whistle and a garbled message be passed - that's if the unreliable thing was working. Any diversion was welcome as driving in the heat caused fatigue and blinking eyelids. So a roadside mug of tea brewed up in a mess tin on an improvised stove fuelled by petrol saturated sand in a can was always welcome.

It was a good idea to keep alert as hostile Arabs delighted in driving in the middle of the road bent over the wheel of beaten-up trucks belching clouds of black smoke. It was a case of who blinks first! These road hogs were a real hazard especially as units reported attempts to force their cable cutting patrol jeeps off the road.

On the road it was usually blistering hot during the afternoon with the sun still as hot as a furnace due to the sun beating down and the air as dry as a bone. All right for those lucky enough to be cooling off in the sea, sun bathing or otherwise enjoying their stay in Egypt but not pleasant for the long haul drivers.

I recall requisitioning Royal Army Service Corps (RASC) trucks and their drivers for long hauls. They would arrive and looking at the state of some of the drivers I'd think 'What a shower', until I learned that they were always on the move. Seldom getting rest with a roof over their head in a camp and often sleeping beneath their trucks. They were heroes.

Drivers when driving along desert tracks would occasionally report seeing robed camel drovers either walking slowly across the desert or lying prostate on the sand with their camels nearby. Others purified themselves before prayers by washing with sand if no water was available. They then kneeled while repeatedly lowering their forehead to prayer mats and raising their face to the sky. They were obviously devout Muslims facing Mecca while reciting Koranic verses as they prayed to Allah, which they did five times a day wherever they might be. They prayed at dawn before sunrise, midday after the sun had passed its highest point, during the afternoon before sunset, in the evening after sunset and finally during the night.

The drover's job was to lead the first camel by a rope tied to a peg attached to its nose, with each of the other camels of the file being led by the camel in front of it connected by a similar rope. Deeper in the Sinai drivers passed nomads with cotton shemagh head-dresses wrapped around their heads leading mule trains; some no doubt carrying contraband that they'd been paid to shift.

Apart from the heat, MT drivers had to contend with the fog of sandstorms and dusty windscreens spattered with dead flies. If they were unfortunate enough to travel closely behind another truck they encountered plumes of dust kicked up by its tyres adding to their discomfort.

Dark storm clouds could sometimes be seen either drifting or seemingly racing across the Mediterranean sky. Then suddenly a violent crack of thunder would sound and heavy rain would be apparent, at first spattering the parched desert sand and then hammering down in a torrent.

Night comes quickly in the desert and before long it is pitch black and too dangerous to drive on some of the crumbling stony tracks. So it's up with the bivouacs, brew-up and head down wrapped in a blanket for the night.

Nature at work

At night the peace was disturbed by the song of nocturnal male crickets trying to attract females with their loud persistent chirping and the sound of jackals howling echoed. By day overhead the occasional falcon could be seen soaring while scanning the expanse below for prey onto which it might suddenly dive and lift it away clutched in its claws as they do in the UK. The desert is, after all, home to a variety of lizards, snakes and scorpions.

But the notorious 'shitehawk', a derogatory term used by soldiers in place of the correct name 'black kite', preferred an easier means of getting their food. They were despised for their habit of stealing food. They'd swoop down and clear your plate or snatch a sandwich from your hand if you weren't careful (as do UK seaside town seagulls). So when eating outside you'd need to wave your arms over the food continuously between each mouthful. But when overflying the desert they have an uncanny ability to locate carrion and dozens would swoop onto the carcase leaving only bare bones.

Big black cockroach
Source: www.bugguide.net © 2013 Sean McVey

Whenever food became available there was always something ready to devour it. I recall treading on a huge black flying 'shit' beetle and squashing it, as we did to the many cockroaches we came across. Within a minute or so a disciplined army of ants would appear in a column to carry the precious food underground.

23

OBEDIENCE TO AUTHORITY

Survival rations remain intact

As any serviceman or woman will know, 'obedience' is the act of obeying. Being obedient implies submissive behaviour and the need to conform to the wishes or direction of an authority figure such as an officer or NCO.

While studying Social Psychology I needed to learn about Stanley Milgram's experiments on 'compliance', one of which involved two people. An unsuspecting subject acted as a 'teacher' whose behaviour was being observed and a 'learner' who was an accomplice of the experimenter. The 'teacher' would operate apparatus connected to an 'electric chair' with switches labelled from 'slight shock' to 'severe shock' and outputs increasing from 15v to 450v in 15-volt increments.

Before the learning task commenced, the teacher received a specimen low voltage shock to illustrate the punishment awarded to the 'learner' for an incorrect answer. The teacher had seen the learner being strapped into the electric chair in the next room and believed the shocks could be painful.

Then the teacher standing by the power unit was instructed to monitor the learner's learning task. Each time the learner made an error the teacher was to administer a shock that was to be increased in severity with every error made. As the voltages were increased the teacher became distressed because he could hear the learner screaming as if in intense pain. (In truth no shocks were applied but the teacher didn't know this). At 300 volts the learner started kicking the wall after which there was silence.

Experimenter (the Authority Figure):
'Incorrect answer - Ignore the screaming - Increase the voltage'

At this point the experimenter instructed the teacher to treat 'no response' as an incorrect answer and to increase the voltage accordingly. The majority of teachers continued until the 450-volt (severe shock) mark even though the learner was silent (apparently unconscious or dead). Some teachers asked the experimenter to stop the experiment when the screaming started, but the experimenter insisted they carry on, causing great suffering.

While military orders and discipline must be paramount, Milgram's experiment showed that 'obedience to authority' is a powerful influence on a person's behaviour, particularly if those who direct do so from a position of power or authority. Many people do not know how to disobey white-coated or other authority figures or are unwilling to do so even when placed in challenging situations such as the L/Cpl's dilemma outlined below.

Landing craft goes aground

During October and November 1952 there were Brigade and Divisional Exercises in the southern half of the Canal Zone. Accordingly, on one occasion in order to save track-wear, the 1st Battalion Support Company carriers aboard landing craft were moved south down the Suez Canal. Unfortunately, one of the craft went aground in the Great Bitter Lake and remained there for 24 hours. The only food available to the Lance Corporal and guardsmen on board was a box of emergency rations that could endure time and weather. It contained ready to eat concentrated tinned survival rations such as Irish stew, high calorific value snacks and chocolate, nutritional drink compounds with water purification tablets, tea and sugar. A box was carried on every vehicle. But when the party got ashore the rations were found to be intact, because written on the boxes was the words: 'To be opened only on the authority of an Officer'.

The 1st Battalion's CO, Lieutenant Colonel Richard Crichton MC later commented, *'They were well disciplined but very hungry Coldstreamers!'*

24

Return to UK

Coronation Parade in UK

In May 1953 five officers and a lucky group of 100 other ranks were flown to the United Kingdom in order to participate in the Coronation Parade. They returned to El Ballah in mid-June. But good news was to follow shortly afterwards. The 1st Battalion Welsh Guards was due to relieve us in early September 1953 and this time it wasn't a rumour, it was true.

Setting sail for Liverpool

On 11th September 1953 the main body of the 1st Battalion Coldstream Guards embarked in HMT *Empire Halladale* at Port Said and set sail for Liverpool. But what a rough passage it had due to storms in the Bay of Biscay. The seas were mountainous lifting the propeller shaft out of the sea and causing the engine to race. The bow was dipping and rising alarmingly and the ship rolling into the deep troughs. Looking over the side at one instant nothing could be seen but a mountain of sea and next, nothing but sky.

Some were too seasick to worry about the storm. But like many others I was absolutely terrified just like the disciples aboard a fishing-boat when there arose a great storm with waves threatening to engulf the boat. I'm pretty sure that others like me were mumbling the wonderful seafarers' hymn *'Eternal Father strong to save, whose arm hath bound the restless wave'* and praying that He would save us.

I count myself lucky to have made it home safely as I'd been appointed Troop Deck Sergeant. I had the unenviable task of ensuring the troop deck was in pristine condition for the Ship Captain's Rounds - a thorough Inspection of the ship at 1000 hours daily. So preparations before rounds entailed detailing four guardsmen to grab each corner of a blanket and confiscate everything that was not in authorised locations.

Favourite places to 'hide' articles were behind pipes and fittings or under bunks. This meant that packs of cards, cigarettes, books, papers, you name it, ended up in the blanket; which was then placed in the luggage hold on the same deck. Stuff could be reclaimed when the hold was opened in the evening. I was careful to avoid a 'mishap' or accidental 'man over board' whilst on the upper deck.

But we made it and disembarked at Liverpool on 23rd September 1953 where we handed in our weapons, were paid, given a railway warrant and sent on well-earned leave, thereby ending our Suez Canal Zone encounter.

A very brief summary of events following posting to Windsor is given below.

Victoria Barracks Windsor

The main body reassembled at Victoria Barracks, Windsor toward the end of October 1953 where Duty Companies mounted the Windsor Castle Guard and undertook street-lining duties followed by additional Public Duties in London. Several months later there were the usual drill and rehearsals for the Queen's Birthday Parade.

After enjoying a wonderful leave I rejoined the Battalion early in order to organise the unit transport. A fleet of brand new Austin 1 ton trucks complete with a compliment of trailers were to be issued from a vehicle ordnance depot. After arranging to collect the trucks a party of drivers led by an NCO set off to pick up the vehicles. Regrettably on the way back to Windsor powerful headlights of traffic approaching the convoy had dazzled the lead driver. Then bang, bang, bang. Each of the entire group of trucks crashed into the trailer in front and did considerable damage.

Crashed Austin 1 tonner

I was not pleased and spent ages filling in FMT1 accident reports and the Transport Officer and Commanding Officer both signalled their displeasure!

Training reservists

Brigade of Guards Reservists were required to attend a two-week period of updating and refresher training each year so that they would be efficient and effective should it be necessary to recall them for duty with the Colours.

Accordingly the 1st Battalion was called upon to train about 1 000 Officers and Other Ranks based in the Stanford Training Area.

Originally designated as a battle area there were large tracts of gorse covered sandy heath located 7 miles north of Thetford. If my memory serves me right I think we were housed in Nissen Huts at West Tofts Camp that had a nearby assault course and ranges for live firing.

The other camp where I spent my some of my stint was Bodney South. That's where my NCOs took groups of reservists on maintenance and driver training while I chose the motorcyclist's option. That was a bad decision because due to my arrogance it led to a shameful outcome.

The ex. Signals Platoon despatch riders were required to ride the heavy BSA 500s over an obstacle course that included crossing a small stream with short steep banks on either side. Riders were able to cross it, but with difficulty. It took a bit of courage to attempt it and one rider complained to me as I stood watching the action from a nearby bridge, 'My bike's got no guts. It'll never climb up the bank.'

'Nonsense,' I said feeling that being a sergeant I was invincible. 'I'll show you how to do it.'

Mistake! I got on the bike and rode it down the slippery bank, across the water and part way up the opposite bank when disaster struck. The engine cut out and I rolled backward down the bank losing control and ending up in the water beneath the bike. This resulted in much laughter from the reservists observing from the bridge and loss of face for me. Terribly embarrassing.

A few days later three sergeants climbed aboard my clapped out 1931 Standard 'Big Nine' saloon that I'd bought for £20 and we set of for a night out in a pub near Downham Market. All was going well until suddenly a loud knocking noise was emanating from the engine.

'Oh dear chaps. Can't go far tonight.'

We had a drink in the nearest pub and I managed to get the car back to camp where the following morning I removed the sump only to find that an aluminium connecting rod had broken in two. As the engine rotated with the piston stuck up the bore, the rod went bang bang bang against the cylinder block but luckily the big end remained intact. I was fortunate when the next day I found a similar engine at a scrap yard in Kings Lynn and removed a conrod that cost me 10 shillings. I fitted the conrod and the old banger ran sweetly once again. But the car was going to get me in trouble later after I returned to Windsor.

Lakenheath United States Air Force base was only a few miles away and one evening our WO's & Sgt's Mess members were invited as their guests to a meal with their equivalently ranked aircrews. They treated us wonderfully well and it was the first and only time I had a massive 'T' bone steak and plenty of wine. The Yanks knew how to live well.

Returning to Victoria Barracks

At the conclusion of the reservist-training phase I returned to Victoria Barracks in the old car with a trunk strapped to the luggage rack stuffed with pheasants. It was no use shooting rabbits because the population was ravaged with myxomatosis, a fatal viral disease.

About the car

Leaving the Victoria Barracks Sgt's Mess one dark evening I drove slowly without lights alongside the square toward the stables where I parked overnight. My battery was almost flat and I didn't want trouble but nevertheless I got it! Suddenly a stentorian roar was heard above the loud exhaust note. It was the RSM shouting, 'Sgt Walklin. Here!'

I stopped the car, got out and doubled over to him. Pulled my feet in and said, 'Yes Sir.'

'You're on a charge. Driving across the square without lights contrary to Standing Orders.' He then strode to his bungalow quarters.

Next day at Company Orders, 'March in' Charge read out. RSM gives evidence.

'Well Sgt Walklin, what have you to say?' enquired the Company Commander.

'Sir, I'd detected a short circuit in the fuse box located directly beneath the gravity fed petrol tank on the bulkhead. So I thought it would be unwise to switch on the lights for fear of causing a fire in barracks. I therefore drove very slowly to a place of safety. There were no personnel other than the RSM in the vicinity.'

'Very sensible Sgt Walklin, but please ensure that the defect is rectified before driving the vehicle again. "Seen".'

I felt that being such a young SNCO I wasn't rated by the RSM who'd earlier charged me with 'Mowing the lawn in an irregular manner'.

I did my share of Public Duties too even though Transport Sergeants were not often considered for Sergeant of the Guard duties. However I was.

The photograph taken at Windsor Castle during Easter 1954 shows the Officer of the Guard inspecting the guard with me following him.

Move to Chelsea Barracks

On 1st March 1955 the Battalion was posted to Chelsea Barracks, London where it carried out Public Duties at the Royal Palaces, the Tower and the Bank of England.

Inspecting the Windsor Castle Guard Easter 1954

Once again I did my bit but due to my shorter stature my guard duties were confined to Tower Main or Tower Spur and Bank of England Piquet. The Royal Palaces were the domain of the taller NCOs and guardsmen.

The Bank Piquet

During the 18th Century a detachment of Foot Guards defended the Bank and for about 200 years Royal Guardsmen in their scarlet tunics stood sentry outside the Bank of England on Threadneedle Street. Known as the Bank Piquet the detachment guaranteed the security of the vaults and conveyed a strong message of authority.

One day in 1955 I was detailed as the Sergeant of the Bank Piquet and together with the Officer of the Guard, JNCOs, guardsmen from my Transport Platoon and a drummer carrying a lantern we mounted guard at 1500 hours and marched in scarlet tunics and bearskins through Pimlico and along The Embankment to the Bank.

On arrival at the Bank we made our way to the Guardroom walking on red carpets specially laid each evening on the marble floor in order to avoid damage caused by hob nailed boots. Duties were allocated and sentries posted for the 13-hour night-guard. As was the custom, the Officer of the Guard was given a bottle of port wine and could invite a friend or two to dinner in the Bank. I received two shiny new shillings, the others got one new shilling each.

During the early evening the Officer of the Piquet summoned me to meet him in the corridor where I soon had the good fortune to be introduced to Sir Winston Churchill who'd been invited to dine with the Governor of the Bank of England and the Officer of the Piquet.

Sir Winston mumbled something quite unintelligible to me as I saluted and I thought that perhaps he had topped up with a glass of champagne and whisky and soda before arriving.

After the guests' meal I was invited to join the Officer to finish off the port that I found most enjoyable. But opted to withdraw when I felt my speech beginning to slur.

Guards Battalions continued to mount the Bank Piquet until the evening of 31st July 1973 when it was discontinued.

On another occasion the Bank Piquet was sprayed with liquid from a fire extinguisher aimed by a student passing in a coach travelling along the Embankment. This stained and damaged some of our tunics but the offender didn't get away with it because I'd memorised the registration number and reported it to the Metropolitan Police. The student was subsequently charged with *'Obstructing the Queen's Guard in the execution of their duties.'* The offender paid a heavy price for his misconduct.

Chelsea flower showground

My responsibilities as the Transport Sergeant also included regularly mowing the lawns and grassy areas of the Royal Hospital Chelsea and Chelsea Flower Showground located close to Chelsea Barracks.

Ferguson Tractor outside Transport Office, Chelsea Barracks

I didn't personally mow the grass but I did need to ensure that the tractor was regularly maintained. After each service I'd 'road test' it around the barracks to check that everything worked before handing it over to the guardsman groundsman. The photograph was taken outside the Transport Office.

The cricket fan revisited

Although a relatively junior sergeant while at Chelsea Barracks I sometimes found myself lumbered with the role of Acting Company Sergeant Major HQ Company. This task usually fell to me during Bank Holidays or key leave periods when the seniors somehow managed to dodge the job.

One morning I was managing the Company Orders parade. This involved liaising with the Sgt-in-Waiting, lining up those ordered to attend and marching them in before the Company Commander.

I knocked his office door, opened it and entered saluting the eloquently attired gentleman dressed in Guards Officers off duty wear. There was he standing beside his desk leaning on a tightly rolled umbrella. I noted his smart City outfit. White shirt and Brigade tie beneath his conservatively cut jacket, pinstriped trousers, and shiny black shoes topped with a black bowler. The tightly rolled umbrella, which would never be unfurled rain or shine, completed his splendiferous appearance.

Turning to me he asked, 'What have we today, Sgt Walklin?'

'Four on report and one application, Sir. The charges have been entered in the red book on your desk.'

Still upright but now standing at right angles to the desk he ordered, 'Right let's get on with it.'

I opened the door and ordered the Sgt-in-Waiting to march-in the first case and the NCO who'd give evidence.

'March in left right left.' ordered the Sgt-in-Waiting.

Then I pick up command. 'Arms in. Mark time. Halt. Left turn.'

Gdsm Bloggs is now facing the desk as I read out the charge.

The Company Commander listens and while the evidence is being given there is the Major holding his umbrella pointed end upwards, making repeated "forward defensive strokes" with his improvised cricket bat. Next a "stroke to leg!"

'What have you to say Gdsm Bloggs?' the Company Commander asks while continuing his stroke play.

'Permission to speak, Sir. Please.'

'Yes, please.' mumbles the Company Commander, after which Gdsm Bloggs is allowed to speak.

'Blah blah blah.'

Punishment is announced and stooping over the table the Company Commander signs up the report book.

'Fall-in. Left turn. Quick march. Left right left....' and the offender rapidly exits the office.

Major Richard Carr Gomm OBE Croix de Guerre

The HQ Company Commander was none other than the officer labelled 'cricket-mad' whilst at El Ballah. A perfect gentleman, he was improperly and cruelly belittled by a number of spiteful soldiers using the derogatory term 'Scar Gomm' when talking about him. OK, while he was thought of as being something of an unusual character, there is no doubt of his bravery and commitment to the Regiment.

Since leaving the Regiment I'd taken an interest in this officer born in 1922 and learned that he had attended Stowe where he enjoyed cricket and won a place at Oriel College, Oxford. But when the 2nd World War was declared he declined the place at Oxford and although only 17 years old he enlisted in the Royal Berkshire Regiment. [4]

4. My school pals and others from my hometown Reading were drafted into the 'Berks.'

He was a descendent of Field Marshal Sir William Gomm GCB who had fought at Waterloo and he too looked forward to joining the family regiment. So in 1941 he did so, transferring to the Coldstream Guards where he hoped to become the second member of the family to become a field marshal.

Commissioned in the 4th (Armoured) Battalion Coldstream Guards he was appointed Troop Commander of 2 Squadron and saw action commanding a Churchill tank from the beaches of Normandy, during the push through Germany and on to the gates of Belsen Concentration Camp. Shell shrapnel leaving nasty scars to his face and eye twice wounded him. He was awarded the Croix de Guerre and mentioned in despatches.

If only those disrespectful men who'd ridiculed him due to the disfigurement on his face knew the truth maybe they'd have refrained from demeaning him.

Caring for the deprived

While returning from Egypt through Europe by train, he stopped to visit the Turin Shroud and came across a street full of lonely and destitute old people and handicapped children. He was saddened by what he saw and once back in UK he wondered how the elderly were treated in Britain.

Attending a Billy Graham crusade at Harringay prompted him to dedicate his life and wealth to helping others. Perhaps he had heard and taken to heart the words of Jesus given in Mathew 19:24 *'Again I tell you it is easier for a camel to pass through the eye of a needle than for a rich man to enter the kingdom of God.'*

I recall the shockwaves passing through the Battalion as rumours of his resignation in November 1955 and decision to work as an unpaid home help rapidly spread.

While doing this work he became known as *'the scrubbing major'* but he persisted and lived long enough to set up the Carr-Gomm Society and win prizes for *'Lifetime achievement in caring for the elderly'* and for *'Outstanding lifetime devotion to providing help and accommodation for the lonely across Britain and abroad'*.

A decent God fearing gentleman he died aged 86 in 2008.

I too left the Regiment in November 1955 upon completion of a month's pre-release course as heavy goods fitter at H&G

Simonds Brewery back in my hometown, Reading. Colonel Crichton wrote my 'Final Assessment of Conduct and Character and Testimonial.'

Final Assessments of Conduct and Character

(To be completed personally by the Commanding Officer)

Military Conduct Exemplary

Testimonial (To be completed with a view to civil employment)

A hardworking and reliable man who is always willing and interested in his work. He is a good driver and he has a sound mechanical knowledge. He is an able instructor. He has a very pleasant and cheerful personality and he is thoroughly honest, trustworthy and sober.

The above assessments have been read to me.
Signature of Soldier SWalklin.

Place LONDON.

[illegible signature]
(Signature of C.O.) Lieut-Colonel, Commanding,

Date 20 Oct 55 1st Bn. Coldstream Guards. Unit

My final act was to collect my demob outfit from a demobilisation centre. The civilian clothes included a felt trilby hat, a double-breasted pinstripe three-piece 'demob' suit, two shirts with matching collar studs, a tie, shoes and a raincoat. Then I was a civilian until recalled for the 1956 Suez Crisis.

25

THE 3RD BATTALION COLDSTREAM GUARDS MOVE FROM TRIPOLI TO THE CANAL ZONE

During the period 1951-1954 there was an 80 000 strong British Garrison stationed in the Canal Zone. Its purpose being to defend the Canal Zone and the military depots there. Sadly, servicemen and women came under sustained guerrilla attack from local fanatics and Police Auxiliaries.

Active service status

As a result, from 16th October 1951 until the Canal Zone was evacuated on 19th October 1954 personnel serving there were categorised as being 'on active service'. Many lives were lost and it was an unpleasant and dangerous period throughout which terrorist attacks on camps and convoys were frequent occurrences.

The terrorists were evil sadists mouthing curses and threats against the unwelcome occupiers of their land. They'd lie in wait near villages, towns and civilian establishments and from ambush they'd watch in secret for victims. They'd wait to catch their prize then torture and murder the wretched innocent whom they'd targeted, their cries for help going unheard because there'd be nobody nearby to save them.

Added to this was sabotage, abductions of individual servicemen and murders. Many went missing and were never found. The dark wings of death had claimed them. More than 400 HM Forces personnel became casualties together with 126 civilians, married families and children.

Possibly the worse atrocity was the murder on 20th January 1952 of Sister Anthony, an American teacher at St Vincent de Paul's College in Ismailia whom was killed in her Convent. Terrorists had discovered that she had warned the British of an impending ambush on a military convoy.

Agitation against the British

In 1951 the 3rd Battalion was stationed in Tripoli where it was standing by to fly to the Persian Gulf due to the probability of trouble in the oil-fields.

But trouble came from the Egyptians, due to the rise of nationalism and a *Foreign Troops Out* attitude. Nahas Pasha, King Farouk's Prime Minister and leader of the nationalist Waft Party and its paramilitary 'Blue Shirts', had abrogated the 1936 Anglo-Egyptian Treaty causing civil disorder. The resulting violent riots caused an alarmed King Farouk to urge activists to stop agitating and sacked Pasha that restored relative calm. But in July 1952 Nasser overthrew the corrupt regime.

As a result of the violence, reinforcements were sent to safeguard British interests. Up to 6 000 British troops from the 1st Infantry Division, which included the 3rd Battalion Coldstream Guards, 3rd Battalion Grenadier Guards and 1st Battalion The Cameron Highlanders arrived in the Canal Zone of Egypt.

It was the last phase of what has been described as the biggest airlift of troops since World War II.

Move from Tripoli

Consequently on 2nd November 1951 the 3rd Battalion emplaned in Hastings and Valetta aircraft and flew from Castel Benito Airfield, Tripoli to Fayid in order to help put an end to anti-British disturbances.

The Battalion then travelled overland to Tel-el-Kebir (TEK), where they undertook boring but frequent guard duties along the lengthy perimeter wire and secured searchlight installations. It is possible that some readers will know the feeling!

Into action

Before long, local extremists supported by Cairo students caused a lot of trouble in and around TEK and on 11th January 1952 a train was attacked in Tel-el-Kebir Village Station. The duty platoon rushed to the location and came under heavy fire but held out until reinforced by two 3rd Battalion Companies who promptly occupied the village. Armed terrorists were killed and many taken prisoner but sadly Sgt Copson was killed by a sniper's bullet. The Battalion was also engaged in El Hamada after which it occupied the village.

According to Hansard on 3rd and 4th December 1951, Egyptian auxiliary police opened fire on British soldiers near the water filtration plant outside Suez and killed 11. Then on 18th December 1951, fire from the police station in Ismailia killed a British officer passing in a jeep. And 20 auxiliary police and four terrorists in a lorry attacked a roadblock near Tel-el-Kebir. As a result of this and other attacks the area was cleared. But found in the police station compound of El Hamada were a police major general and 116 armed police as well as quantities of ammunition and other arms.

On 19th January 1952 two British infantrymen were killed. Then on 23rd January, when British casualties had reached 33 killed and 69 wounded and with evidence of attack by the Egyptian auxiliary police, General Erskine was instructed to disarm them.

Caracol and Bureau de Sanitaire fighting

'In Ismailia on the morning of 25th January there were about 400 Egyptian police in the *Caracol*, the regular Police Station and the Governor's Office. A further 600 Egyptian police were in the *Bureau Sanitaire* (a health office) located about 400 yards from the *Caracol.* General Erskine sent a message to the Sub-Governor of Ismailia saying that since the auxiliary police had been firing on our troops as well as helping the terrorists, it was necessary to disarm them and requested him to order them to come out of their barracks without arms. He was told that arms would be restored to the regular police who would then be allowed to continue their duties.

The Sub-Governor replied saying that both the regular and auxiliary police would resist in accordance with their orders from the Egyptian Government. In view of this statement the operations against the *Caracol* and the *Bureau Sanitaire* were put in train.

Loudspeaker vans broadcast requests for police to surrender but at 0656 hours firing by the police started from the *Bureau Sanitaire* and continued with increasing intensity until 0710 hours. The British then retaliated by a tank firing one round of blank as a warning. But the police continued to fire. At 0715 hours the British returned the fire for the first time, six rounds of 20-pounder tank gun shells as well as small arms. This produced a very heavy fusillade from the police.

At 0900 hours British infantry supported by tanks forced their way inside the walled compound of the *Bureau Sanitaire* but our infantry quickly suffered 14 casualties and were withdrawn. At 1000 hours fire was opened again and at 1037 hours surrender started. The British suffered three killed and 13 wounded. The Egyptian police casualties were 41 killed, 73 wounded, and 886 surrendered.'

Based on Hansard report: http://hansard.millbanksystems.com/commons/1952/jan/31/egypt-british-military-action-ismailia

The next day an Australian newspaper printed the following item. *'British troops smashed into Ismailia's police fortress yesterday and forced the main body of the well armed Egyptian police reserves to surrender after a battle lasting all the morning. Twenty-pounder guns of the Centurion tanks pounded the Bureau de Sanitaire, to a smoking mass of bloodstained rubble by midday resulting in well armed police at the Bureau sector of Ismailia surrendering.'*

Apparently a tank of 3 Troop 4 Royal Tank Regiment had fired six shells into the Tower but the Egyptian force still did not surrender. Then all three tanks opened fire and the building collapsed.

Combating terrorism

Then followed a period of manning roadblocks and checkpoints, patrolling desert areas and roads in the triangle between Cairo, Port Said and Port Suez.

There was considerable guerrilla activity around Moascar and Ismailia and pretty well all along the Sweet Water Canal toward Fanara and Suez. Terrorists would ambush convoys on the Treaty Road, bomb passing trucks and open fire on their drivers and escorts. They sniped at patrols from hidden positions behind the banks of the canal and promptly vanished when soldiers approached. This kept the 3rd Battalion Companies busy before moving on 22nd February 1952 from TEK to tented accommodation at Old Basuto Camp, Fanara.

Move to Fanara

Once settled in Fanara the inevitable guard duties, exercises, cable cutting and power line patrols, searches and routine foot and motorised patrols occupied the Battalion. Guard duties were also mounted to prevent the considerable losses of ammunition from the Abu Sultan Depot.

I was delighted to see the wonderful Sgt Rhondda Collins who was at one time my Superintending Sergeant at the Guards Depot. I gave him a wave as I drove my truck into the 3rd Battalion camp at Fanara. There he was, smart as ever, the Regimental Police (Provost) Sergeant on duty at the gate.

The 'O' Force

In order to form a buffer between the Arabs in Aqaba and the Jews in Eilat the 'O' Force was created. This comprised infantry in the form of one company of the 3rd Battalion Coldstream Guards together with a battery of Light AA Artillery and a RAF Ground Detachment. The force located in Jordan was tasked with guarding Aqaba airfield. Each of the three 3rd Battalion duty companies were detached and rotated to undertake this role - a pleasant relief from the Fanara post.

A lucky group of 100 all ranks were flown to UK to participate in the Coronation Parade and finally on Christmas Eve 1953 the 3rd Battalion left the Canal Zone on board HMT *Lancashire* disembarking at Liverpool on 5th January 1954.

26

The 1956 Suez Crisis and the 3rd Battalion

In June 1956 the 3rd Battalion Coldstream Guards occupied Shorncliffe Barracks 2 miles west of Folkestone in Kent where it formed part of the 1st Guards Brigade, 3rd Infantry Division. But it wasn't long before the Egyptians nationalised the Suez Canal and the Suez Crisis began.

During the summer of 1956 while the author, an ex. 1st Battalion Class 'A' reservist was on holiday in Devon he received a telegram instructing him to report within 24 hours to Pirbright Camp in Surrey. He had been recalled to the Colours for the 1956 Suez Crisis and on 9th August joined the 3rd Battalion Coldstream Guards.

The Adjutant, Captain DHA Lewey commenting on the affairs of those affected by recall wrote: *'This disruption was of course common to all ranks and many reservists' families had to move into cheaper accommodation, hand back articles being hire-purchased, and generally accept a lower standard of living. This the men cheerfully accepted so long as they believed they were to be used on active service. Only when this belief was sapped by false alarms and weeks of routine training did they become impatient.'*[5]

Like many others who'd been recalled this was to be a life-changing event. I'd rejoined as a representative to the motor trade and on release joined Gillette Engineering Department where over a lengthy period of time I studied and qualified as a professional Mechanical and Production Engineer. So as a result of the recall fate had again played a hand in my future. But I digress.

We reservists were inoculated, issued with documents, khaki battledress and a kitbag into which we stuffed all our newly issued kit complete with green coated brasses, fresh webbing and packs and hard knobbly 'ammo' boots'. Without wasting any time the reservists were packed off

5. Crichton, Richard (1972) *The Coldstream Guards 1946-1970 p 50*

and sent by rail to Shorncliffe where they joined the regulars in Moores Barracks.

As I write this paragraph tears of pride fall from my eyes. Regarding the mobilisation of reservists the Adjutant commented *'By every train there arrived at Shorncliffe from Pirbright a party of Reservists under their own NCOs, properly dressed in uniform. I have seldom seen anything more heartening than these men's reactions to their recall. They were splendid.'* [6]

The Adjutant and Regimental Sergeant Major (RSM) 'Dougie' Glisson (later to be promoted Major Quartermaster) interviewed every man as he arrived. Soon it was to be my turn and shortly after the interview I was 'marched in' on Commanding Officer's Orders and formally awarded my three chevrons and red sash and appointed Transport Sergeant, Headquarter (HQ) Company. I'd served as Transport Sergeant with the 1st Battalion previously during our 1951 to 1953 tour in MELF3. So having considerable practical experience in the Canal Zone I suppose that is why they appointed me straight from 'Civvy Street'.

It is pleasing to note Captain Lewey's comments *'From the first they [the reservists] were treated in every respect as regular soldiers and were required to turn themselves out like any other guardsman. In a matter of days they became indistinguishable as Reservists except that being a few years older, they tended to behave more sensibly and steadily than the younger regular guardsmen....'* [7]

Preparing the vehicles

The Battalion was on 48 hours notice to deploy to Egypt. This meant that our transport needed to be prepared for the campaign and loaded ready for shipment to Egypt. So our vehicles were camouflaged by painting them in matt Desert Blush that would enable them to be exposed to extreme weather conditions and to blend in with the desert sand.

Regarding the painting operation I was shocked when inspecting the Transport parking area. There I found drivers using brooms to spread pools of yellow paint they'd tipped from five-gallon paint cans over canopies that they'd spread flat on the vehicle park. I was not pleased and gave them a 'bollocking'.

6. Ibid., *p 50*

7. Ibid., *p 50*

'Quicker than paint brushes, Sergeant,' grumbled one of them caught in the act. It took ages for the paint to dry but on reflection I suppose they deserved a bit of praise for using their initiative.

But while on the subject of painting vehicles I recall an incident when the Adjutant appeared intent on monitoring progress. I joined him and we walked toward the first truck finished in the new matt paint complete with smart Regimental signs blue red blue with the Coldstream Star at the centre and divisional signs. I felt quite pleased with the finished job. But the Adjutant, moving on to the next vehicle appeared horrified having spotted a blackened handprint on the bonnet. 'Look at that Sgt Walklin. Can't be seen with vehicles in that state!'

'Well Sir, there's not much we can do about it. If you rub petrol onto the mark it spreads out and is soaked up by the paint. We've tried to prevent making oily marks on the paintwork during routine maintenance but without success.'

'This is not good enough. Have all the vehicles repainted in gloss paint.'

'But Sir, the gloss would make the vehicles shine like mirrors in the desert. Easily spotted.'

'Nevertheless, do as I say. I'll not tolerate sub-standard presentation. Get on with it right away.'

Thankfully the white recognition signs painted on the vehicles in the form of a large 'H' went without a hitch.

Loading and unloading the vehicles

According to plan our heavily laden echelon of fighting vehicles was loaded onto a Landing Ship at Barry Docks in Wales. But subsequently unloaded and returned to Shorncliffe ending the grand strategy i.e. to land on Alexandria beaches as an assault battalion. Then it was load and unload transport again. Sadly and infuriatingly instead of firm decisions by the Ministry of Defence (MOD) planners or other decision makers there were 'It's definitely on,' followed shortly by 'No, false alarm, it's off.' But somehow or other the 3rd Battalion Coldstream Guards advance party, transport and logistics had set sail in two ships for the Mediterranean one ending up in Malta and the other in Gibraltar.

The 3rd Battalion of The Parachute Regiment was parachuted into Egypt and we were now hyped up ready to go and just awaiting the order to move when the British and French forces halted and that was it.

'Release all reservists immediately and stand down.'

What an expensive and embarrassing disaster!

The 3rd Battalion returned to peacetime status and soon after was posted to Germany.

Thanks are due to the late Colonel R J V Crichton CVO MC, a much-admired gentleman, once my Commanding Officer of the 1st Battalion Coldstream Guards, for reference to his researches.

Anxious to learn more about him I discovered that he had seen much action and had been twice wounded. He was educated at Eton, attended Sandhurst and was commissioned into the Coldstream Guards in 1936.

On the evening of 14th May 1940, shortly before the withdrawal of the BEF, 1st Battalion Coldstreamers occupied slit trenches on a Belgian canal bank, each company with a platoon on the far side to act as an outpost. Well-armed German troops mounted in motorcycle sidecars appeared and four were killed, causing German artillery to open fire on the Coldstreamers.

Orders were given to withdraw but when Lieutenant Crichton crossed the canal with two men to organise withdrawal of the No 3 Company outpost, the enemy had already penetrated its defences. He attacked with grenades and got the men back across the canal and was awarded an MC for this act of bravery.

He was severely wounded in the action almost losing an arm and was in and out of hospital for almost two years before returning to active service with the 3rd Battalion in the Italian Campaign.

He was appointed No 2 Company Commander in November 1943 to prepare for the first battle of Monte Camino in February 1944. He was wounded again at Trimonsuoli but returned from hospital a month later.

On 30th June, his Company entered Montepulciano as advance guard of the battalion. Large shells hitting the area caused casualties but he escaped unharmed and fought with his Company all the way to Florence and was mentioned in dispatches.

So I reckon we were very lucky to have such an experienced officer initially as our 1st Battalion Second in Command while in the Canal Zone and later as our CO.

27

Absent friends

A long-term Canal Zoner friend, once Pte Ray Applin, 3rd Battalion The Parachute Regiment (sometimes referred to as 'the Scruffy 3rd'), comes to lunch each Wednesday and our conversation inevitably centres on vintage motorbikes, classic cars and our times in the Canal Zone during the 1950s. But always before the forthcoming Remembrance Sunday we remember our dear comrades, some of whom have passed but many others dear to us whom we've lost contact with. No doubt many readers, even after 60 odd years, will feel the same. I know how very much my Coldstreamer friends meant to me and I've never forgotten members of my platoon.

Why should anyone cling to such memories after all this time? For Ray it was the brotherhood of mates who'd served and lived together, all having endured the arduous Parachute Regiment training. This closeness extended to the respect and cohesiveness shared among other parachute units such as the USA 82nd. Airborne Para, the 101st Screaming Eagles and the French elite Regiments Estranger de Parachutistes with whom Ray trained.

Referring to the recent spate of TV programmes on Para, RM Commando and Special Forces training, our thoughts turned to our youth and we'd nod and agree, 'Yeah. I did that etc. etc. And I'm sure that a good many currently serving and old soldiers were doing the same.

Our thoughts moved on to how when we joined HM Forces our self-concept changed from a 'civvy' outlook to a military one faced with new responsibilities. Suddenly thrust into uniform we were required to learn about weapons and killing. It seems likely that most of us had no experience in situations involving obedience at any cost with a high probability of being killed. In consequence this caused problems among some recruits who became confused about whether they were simply civilians wearing a military uniform or a real military person.

But somehow we learned the meaning of obedience and conformity.

We fondly recalled the layout of our barrack rooms, the 30 beds, the small fireplace at the end, coal scuttle, burnished fire buckets, broom handles scraped clean with a razor blade, the lockers and kit inspections. But most importantly the rapport and mutual support we gave and received from our mates. Yes, this interdependency was really something that supported us throughout. And this was the foundation for our posting and service in our respective units and of our lifelong fondness for our oppo's. In fact this learning and experience has lasted a lifetime.

Ray confessed that being demobbed and finding himself on a railway station platform devoid of his many Para mates created a void that he couldn't fill for more than a year. Having shared the service brotherhood with constant companions and then finding oneself a loner reinforces the shared support available in HM Forces and the reason why he like me still miss our youthful pals.

Fatalities

For the 3rd Battalion Coldstream Guards the New Year in Tel-El-Kebir was not a time to celebrate. On New Year's Eve 1951 Gdsm J Oldridge was killed by an accidental discharge. On 2nd January 1952 Sgt F Copson was killed by sniper fire and the following day Support Company WO2 (CSM) Christer MM and Staff Sgt (CQMS). F Brown both died in a tent fire. These four are buried in Moascar.

Three others lost their lives during 1952/3, L/Sgt M Talbot who was shot in the neck, L/Cpl J G Stafford and Gdsm R W Lambert who are buried in Fayid.

A Grenadier Guardsman on guard duty was also killed while following terrorists across a minefield around Tel-el-Kebir.

The Regimental Collect

'Eternal Lord, beside whom there is no God, keep we pray Thee the Coldstream Guards second to none in loyal duty to Thine only begotten Son, our Lord Jesus Christ, who with Thee, O Father, and with the Holy ghost, liveth and reigneth, one God, world without end. Amen.'

Tribute to fallen Suez Veterans

In a tribute to the memory of those who didn't return from Egypt Suez Veteran Tony Tolan penned the following poem.

Far away in a foreign land
They pitched their tents in the desert sand
Oh, so young, were these brave men
Never to see their homes again.
That heat, disease, and then the foe
Would take young Bill, and Fred and Joe.
Three long years this war went on,
So many souls were dead and gone.
Soldiers, Sailors, Airmen, and civilians too,
Commonwealth troops to name a few.
We will remember them with pride,
It was for all of us they died.

http//www.suezcanalzone.com/roh_intro.html

At the going down of the sun - we will remember them

28

Canal Zoners Brotherhood

Long live the Canal Zoners brotherhood that ties us together and seals the bond that many of the survivors still share today. Recruits like me feared failure throughout basic training but were driven by the awesome drill sergeants to be among the best. I was later privileged to serve with these men from whom I drew inspiration. Soldiering with them, on active service in the Canal Zone, like many of you readers each with their own role models, gave me confidence and I feel made me a better soldier than I might otherwise have been. No better nor worse than any other serviceman I served with.

No doubt this brotherhood will exist long after I'm gone and it's a pity that we, the 'Forgotten Army', were ignored for about 50 years and it was only due to the persistence of Dame Annette Brooke DBE OBE MP, Lindsay Hoyle MP and many other constituency MPs that the General Service Medal with Canal Zone clasp was eventually grudgingly awarded.

In order to 'pressure' HM Government to seriously address the issue, Lindsay Hoyle MP put forward a motion, *'That this House pays tribute to British military service personnel who served in the Suez Canal Zone between 1951 to 1954; notes that over 300 British servicemen were killed during this period in addition to many others who were tortured; further notes that those service personnel who served during this period have received no form of recognition for their duties and sacrifices made; welcomes the establishment of the Committee headed by Sir Charles Guthrie to review the case for a medal to be awarded; and calls on the Committee and Ministry of Defence to make an announcement as soon as possible.'*

The Canal Zoners did their bit struck in the desert.

Dame Annette Brooke DBE OBE then a Liberal Democrat MP also put forward a motion, *'That this House is concerned that despite many representations over the years, there is no award of a 'Suez Medal' for those who served during the 1951 to 1954 emergency; notes that the Royal British*

Legion passed a resolution at its annual conference earlier this year urging its National Council to use its influence with the Ministry of Defence on this matter; and calls on Her Majesty's Government to invite the Committee on the Grant of Honours, Decorations and Medals to reconsider their policy, not merely relying on the past history of why it was not granted but to make sure that due recognition with equality of treatment is given to this group of servicemen whilst at least some are still alive.'

Had it not been for caring MPs such as these, those who served in the Canal Zone during the set period wouldn't have received a well earned medal. But those serving in the 1956 Suez Crisis were out of luck.

29

Reflecting on the handling of the Suez Crisis

The handling of the Suez Crisis by Prime Minister Anthony Eden was clearly a disaster. As the months went by following the nationalisation of the Suez Canal, Eden took control of foreign policy. This was highlighted by him summoning the then Foreign Secretary, Selwyn Lloyd, to return overnight from New York, where he was negotiating with the Egyptian Foreign Minister, only to immediately fly out with Eden to France to meet the French Prime Minister Guy Mollet.

At that meeting Eden confirmed that if an Anglo-French clandestine agreement that Israel would attack Egypt took place, Britain would intervene militarily on the Canal with France. This momentous decision was taken with no time for the Foreign Secretary to be advised by officials of the consequences of denying any prior involvement for relations with the United States and the Arab world.

Given that the resulting military operation (Operation Musketeer) itself had been completely successful, political pressure from the United States obliged the British and French governments to accept ceasefire terms drawn up by the United Nations.

While accepting a United Nations Emergency Force to replace the Anglo-French presence, Nasser nevertheless ensured the Canal could not be used by sinking or otherwise disabling 47 vessels and floating cranes, thereby successfully blocking with wrecks the channel between Port Said and Port Suez. The Egyptians also destroyed two bridges by blowing up the El Firdan railway bridge and the pontoon bridge at the southern end of Lake Timsah, adding to the obstacles preventing movement of shipping. This meant that merchant ships and oil tankers were trapped between the wrecks, unable to move.

The 'Cease Fire' became effective at midnight on 7th November 1956 and armed forces, salvage operations and mine clearance in the approaches to the Suez Canal were handed over to the United Nations.

Anglo-French forces were withdrawn by 22nd December, when the United States threatened to devalue the British currency and the Prime Minister called a ceasefire, without Israeli or French officials being notified. This caused France to doubt the reliability of the British.

Oh dear, what a distressing event!

30

60 YEARS AGO - THE SUEZ CRISIS

Patricia Jezzard, President of the Suez Canal Zone Veterans Organisation, generously provides the following summary of the matters leading up to the 1956 Suez Emergency and the subsequent events and outcomes. The text results from the many hours she devoted to researching and writing up the following important historical account.

On 13th June 1956 the last British Troops left Egypt under the terms of the Anglo-Egyptian Agreement of 1954. Five day later President Nasser raised the Egyptian flag over the Port Said Navy House as his jet fighters flew overhead and a frigate fired a 21-gun salute. He then gave a heart-rending speech to a cheering crowd and celebrations began to mark to end of foreign occupation of Egyptian soil. Nasser was completing the purchase of Soviet made aircraft, tanks and arms from Czechoslovakia, which might help him to realise one of his goals, the destruction of Israel.

Israel was worried by Egypt's growing military power, the British government humiliated and the French angered by Egypt's new interference in French-ruled Algeria.

When the call for the supply of more arms came from both Egypt and Israel, both Britain and America refused. So Egypt looked to Russia who obliged which incited anger within America as Egypt was obviously drifting away from the West and being influenced by the Soviets.

Despite anti-western demonstrations in Egypt, in January 1956 the United States and Britain had pledged funding to help finance the construction of a new High Dam at Aswan. The US, however, became convinced that the Dam project would not be a success and wanted to reduce expenditure on foreign aid. It was also concerned about Nasser's purchase of Soviet arms.

On 19th July, US Secretary of State John Foster Dulles informed the Egyptian ambassador in Washington that his government had decided that it would not provide the funding. The British foreign secretary, Selwyn Lloyd, followed suit and withdrew the British offer. The World Bank then refused to advance Egypt a promised $200 million. Eden, who recalled Britain's appeasement of Adolf Hitler in the 1930s, looked to military action that might result in Nasser's downfall and restore Britain's influence in the region. The United States, however, made it clear that unjustified military action would not be tolerated.

On 26th July 1956 Gamal Abdul Nasser, President of Egypt, addressed a huge crowd in Alexandria announcing his intention to nationalise the Anglo/French Suez Canal Company declaring that he would take the revenue from the canal ($30+ million per year) to finance his dam. In that speech Nasser chose to delve back even further into history, in a long digression on the building of the Suez Canal a century earlier. That gave him the chance to mention the name of the Frenchman who had built the canal, Ferdinand de Lesseps. This he did at least 13 times. 'De Lesseps', it turned out, was the code word for the Egyptian army to start the seizure, and nationalisation of the Canal.

On 2nd August 1956 the governments of the United States, Great Britain and France summoned an international conference in London to discuss further steps to secure the 'freedom and safety' of the Canal. They considered the Suez Canal an 'international institute', and so they refused to recognize legitimacy of its nationalization. The Anglo-French political and military leadership was determined to restore the colonial status of the Suez Canal by force and they obtained support from Israel. The United States, however, were against the use of force. Eisenhower in particular was concerned for the presidential election due that November, which he intended to win as the incumbent 'peace' president. He knew that the voters would not thank him for taking them into a war in which America had no direct interest.

On 8th August 1956 in London under the command of General Hugh Stockwell was created the Anglo-French staff for planning the war against Egypt. According to its plans, military operations had to be conducted in two stages.

The first stage would start with the advance of the Israeli Army in the Sinai Peninsula in order to contain the main groupings of the Egyptian Army in fights. On the second stage the Anglo-French forces would carry out seaborne landings in Port Said and Port Fouad (Operation *Musketeer)* in order to seize bridgeheads. After concentrating sufficient forces and equipment, they had to advance along the Suez Canal and force Egypt to withdraw its troops from the Canal Zone. Therefore, to the joint Anglo-French fleet, the focal operation of the campaign was the Suez Canal landing operation.

Preparations for the Operation *Musketeer* were thorough and took almost three months. The plan foresaw the following goals. Launching the war by Israel, containing the core of the Egyptian forces in fights in the Sinai Peninsula, massive bombings of the military objects of Egypt, and the combined seaborne and airborne landings.

Much attention was attached to quickly neutralizing the Egyptian airfields. On 5th November 1956 large airborne units had to be parachuted into the zones where they would isolate the sectors of the seaborne landing from the rest of the country. On 6th November at dawn, after a powerful artillery barrage, the main forces had to land on the Egyptian coast. The landing had to apply the tactics of the 'vertical envelopment', it means that within the tactical zone of the coastal defence would land helicopter groups, which would prevent Egyptian troops from moving to the coast. The near objective for the British airborne troops was to seize and hold the Gamil airfield, and for the French troops - to grasp road and railway bridges south of Port Said. Their landing zones were chosen accordingly near their objectives.

From the point of view of the goals of the campaign the place best fit for the seaborne landing was considered the zone of the Suez Canal. So it was decided to disembark the troops in Port Said and Port Fouad. That area constitutes a bridgehead almost completely isolated from the hinterland. It linked with the rest of the country by a narrow, artificial isthmus, whose seizure would make the isolation of landing zones from the rest of Egypt complete. There were two landing sectors designated in the British zone (Port Said), and one in the French zone (Port Fouad). The total front of the seaborne landing stretched over 6 kilometres.

The Israeli's provided a way out. On September 30th a delegation secretly presented the French with a fabricated casus belli: Israel would invade Egypt and race to the Canal. The French and British could then invade, posing as peacekeepers to separate the two sides, and occupy the canal, ostensibly to guarantee the free passage of shipping.

When this plan was presented to Eden he jumped at it. Thus was collusion born. The details were agreed at a secret meeting in Sevres, outside Paris, The British and French forces now had a pretext to invade. For the Israeli's, it would punish Egypt for its escalating incursions into Israel from Gaza. It would also hitch the major European powers to the cause of Israel. Up to that point, the French had tried to be even-handed between Israel and its neighbours while the British had leaned towards the Arab states.

Only a handful of people were let in on the collusion. Most of them thought it was mad from the start, arguing, quite correctly, that the cover for the invasion was so flimsy it would soon be blown. To disguise what was going on the British, in particular, were drawn ever deeper into a bog of lies and deception, particularly with the Americans.

Parliament was also deceived. Both Eden and Selwyn Lloyd, his foreign secretary, told the House of Commons that, as Lloyd put it, *'there was no prior agreement'* with Israel.

The joint Anglo-French headquarters in Cyprus, with Malta also being used, exercised the general command of the invasion. By chance the Mediterranean fleet had assembled at Malta awaiting the First Sea Lords' (Earl Mountbatten) inspection. The British General Charles Keightley became the Commander-in-Chief, and the French Vice-Admiral Pierre Barjot became his deputy. Apart from regular structures, the headquarters had also accommodated a psychological warfare division. There were no Israeli representatives in the headquarters, but the Israeli command followed the general plan of the campaign. It attached a big role to such activities like intelligence and masking.

HMS *Tyne* was to be the Headquarters Ship of the Joint Task Force. Built as a destroyer she was fitted out for her new communications role with the Royal Navy Communication Branch as her main ship's company, supplemented by RAF and Royal Corp of Signals signallers and, later, French personnel.

The British Aircraft Carrier Task Group comprised *Eagle* (as the flag ship), *Albion* and *Bulwark*. All three were to provide air cover and ground strikes, using Sea Hawks, Sea Venoms and Wyverns. The Helicopter Group, *Ocean* (flag) and *Theseus*, were to lift the Royal Marine Commando's ashore on the landing assault.

The First Cruiser Squadron support was *Jamaica* and *Ceylon*. The Daring class ships, *Diana, Duchess, Decoy, Diamond, Defender* and *Daring* joined *Newfoundland.*

The Flotilla comprised *Chieftain, Chaplet* and *Chevron* from the 1st Destroyer Squadron; *Armada, St. Kitts* and *Barfleur* from the 3rd and *Alamein* from the 4th *Cavendish, Comet* and *Contest* of the 6th Squadron were to be in the East Mediterranean.

Whirlwind and *Wizard* of the 5th Frigate Squadron along with *Undine, Ursa* and *Ulysses* from the 5th and *Urania, Crane* and *Modeste* from the 3rd were to be positioned in the Red Sea.

The only British submarine to play a part was HMS/M *Tudor*, which along with the French submarine *La Creole* was to carry out Search and Rescue patrols. Minesweepers from 104th, 105th and 108th Minesweeping Squadrons were engaged with the Minesweeper Support ship *Woodbridge Haven.*

Tankers were made available both for fuel and water, should the water supply be contaminated once ashore (the French even washed out a wine ship for this purpose). Stores and supplies were available but a problem arose in finding an armament supply ship that could carry out transfers at sea. *Retainer* and *Fort Dunvegan* were employed for the replenishment of the three carriers.

While preparing the seaborne landing, British and French air forces conducted systematic reconnaissance. In order to conceal the objectives of the pending operation the reconnaissance enveloped vast areas; practically the whole Mediterranean coast of Egypt. Intelligence also supplied the Anglo-French command with information concerning the Egyptian defence installations in the areas of planned landings. Concentration of the Anglo-French naval force was disguised as common manoeuvres. Originally the areas of concentration were kept secret. But once the secrecy could not be maintained any longer, there were applied demonstrations that had to convince the Egyptians that the seaborne landing would be staged in the vicinity of Alexandria. Many Allied aircraft were painted in yellow and brown colours and bore identification markings of the Egyptian air forces. It was considered indispensable to achieve superiority in forces and equipment. The Anglo-French fleet numbered more than 130 ships, including 7 aircraft carriers, 3 light cruisers, 13 destroyers, 14 patrol boats, 6 submarines, 11 landing crafts, 8 minesweepers, 60 transports and other ships and vessels. The ships were grouped in the Task Force 345, divided into tactical groups of different designations. A minesweeping group was created to make passages in possible minefields.

The Anglo-French air forces possessed 461 aircraft, including 70 bombers, 228 fighters, 81 reconnaissance planes and 82 transport planes. The air forces comprised two bomber wings, one mixed wing, and two transport wings. Moreover, more than 290 aircraft were based on the carriers. Altogether the invading forces had 751 aircraft.

For the landing forces Great Britain had detached an infantry and an armoured division with three infantry brigades plus one airborne brigade, two independent tank regiments, two army artillery groups, an independent armoured regiment, six independent artillery regiments, and three independent infantry battalions. Altogether the British contingent numbered about 45 000 men.

The French forces comprised a mechanised and an airborne division, an independent airborne brigade and an independent tank regiment. Altogether the French contingent numbered more than 20 000 men.

For the helicopter operation was created a separate group comprising two aircraft carriers, *Theseus* and *Ocean,* with 22 helicopters aboard. They had to carry the Commando No.45 of 600 men. They achieved their readiness on 4th October.

While preparing the Suez landing, the Anglo-French command staged in various places of the Mediterranean 10 exercises in seaborne landings with their seaborne and minesweeping forces, and two exercises in airborne landings. Simultaneously the troops were trained in communications. The plan of the operation also foresaw decoy landings, in particular in the Red Sea, near Suez (Operation *Toreador*).

Once the Egyptian command received reliable information about the pending invasion it undertook a number of measures aimed at consolidation of the country's defences. The troops were put on alert, a partial mobilization was announced and the civil population was submitted to military training and service in the popular militia. Yet Egypt's capabilities of repelling the aggression were limited. It lacked professional military cadres and did not have enough modern weapons and equipment.

A seaborne landing at Port Said was deemed unlikely and no defences were organized there. The military equipment, and particularly aircraft, were not dispersed or camouflaged. Out of approx. 200 aircraft, the Egyptian air forces possessed only about half were fit for combat actions. And the lack of trained pilots on the newly acquired Soviet planes was a problem. Nasser moved many of his planes and hid them in Syria, allegedly replacing them with wooden dummies but all 'hits' recorded were actual planes.

At the outbreak of the hostilities the Egyptian Army numbered about 140 000 men, and together with the National Guard and volunteers - 240 000. They were organised in infantry, armoured and artillery brigades. In general in the vicinity of Port Said the Allies enjoyed fivefold superiority over the Egyptians in the troops and absolute superiority in naval and air forces. At the end of October the Allied forces completed their deployment in the Eastern Mediterranean and were ready to start the war.

On 29th October 1956, Israeli paratroopers, led by a zealous officer named Ariel Sharon, were dropped into Sinai to fulfil their side of the bargain. Feigning surprise, the British and French issued an ultimatum to both sides to cease fire. When the Egyptians rejected this, British and French planes based in Cyprus started bombing the Egyptian Air Force on the ground during the night of 31st October.

However, it soon became apparent that the night bombing had not been successful as photographic evidence showed targets were missed. At 0520 the planes took off from Cyprus once again, their targets, Kasfareet, Kabrit, Abu Sueir, Fayid, El Firdan and Deversoir. By the end of the day the three Venom squadrons had flown 104 sorties and jointly claimed 59 Egyptian aircraft (mainly MiGs) destroyed on the ground, 11 probable and 37 damaged, along with damage to airfields and hangars. The French F-84Fs flew a total of 75 sorties claiming 16 aircraft (mainly MiGs) destroyed, 9 probable and 4 damaged, along with airfield and hangar damage.

Meanwhile at 0520 the Fleet Air Arm began its assault. Targets were the airfields at Cairo West, Almaza and Inchas. The three aircraft carriers launched 36 *Sea Hawks*, *Sea Venoms* and *Wyverns* with others flying on protection patrols over the carriers. By the end of the day squadrons from the three carriers claimed 80 aircraft destroyed (22 MiGs), 9 probable and 85 damaged. *Seahawks* also bombed the Egyptian block ship *Akka* to prevent it being sunk in the buoyed channel. It had first been seen moored in Lake Timsah but later observed moving erratically to the southern end of the lake. A strike by twelve *Sea Hawks* failed to sink the ship so when seen again under tow by tugs a second strike was called for, this time making a direct hit. Presuming the ship would now sink, the *Sea Hawks* continued to their target at Abu Sueir, not realising that the Egyptians would succeed in towing her to the main channel where she finally sank.

These raids continued throughout the next few days with targets including, not only airfields, but military camps, especially Huckstep Camp east of Cairo which was estimated to have 85 tanks and some 500 vehicles housed there. Gamil Bridge was another target but despite near misses it remained intact until 1620 when bombs were struck 'dart-like' into the bridge with delayed action fuses and one third of the bridge at the west end was destroyed.

On 5th November, the Anglo/French assault on Suez was launched. Soon after dawn 668 men of the 3rd Battalion The Parachute Regiment and 16th Parachute Brigade Tactical Group, dropped onto El Gamil airfield, while 492 French paratroopers landed south of the al-Raswa bridges at Port Fouad. The capture of these bridges would open the road to Suez but the French paratroopers met much opposition by heavy automatic fire. French air support came to their rescue, managing to also set alight two oil tanks in the strike, the smoke of which hung over Port Said for many days.

After 45 minutes, all Egyptian resistance on the airfield had been overcome and Royal Naval helicopters were bringing in supplies and taking away any wounded. With El Gamil secured, the British Paras moved eastwards towards Port Said, meeting their first serious opposition en route. With air support, they overwhelmed the Egyptian forces then stopped and dug in overnight as the beach area of Port Said was to be bombarded the next day during the seaborne landing.

On 6th November, with *Ocean* and *Theseus* fitted out identically to carry any of the 22 helicopters, troops and for the use as hospital ships (75 casualties each), the sea and helicopter borne assault went in. At 0645 with the *Whirlwinds* carrying six Marine Commandos and the *Sycamores* three, the initial assault began with landings on the beachhead near de Lessop's statue. By the end of the day the helicopters had landed a total of 497 troops, 20 tons of equipment, embarked 96 casualties and made 194 deck landings.

The men flying in the *Sycamores* sat on the floor of the helicopter, the one in the middle with six mortar bombs in his lap holding on to the other two, who sat at the edge of the door with legs dangling over the side, each hugging a 3ft long 106mm shell. The *Whirlwinds* had no doors, seats or windows and the six men aboard had few or no handholds but they were able to fit inside the main body of the helicopter. In convoys of six, the helicopters barely touched the ground before the Marines had jumped clear.

At 0430 the LVTs assault crafts, *Striker* and *Reggio* carrying the 40 Commando landed at Red Beach and *Suvla* and *Anzio* with 42 Commando at Green Beach.

At 0508 the 14 tanks of 'C' Squadron 6th RTR prepared to leave *Rampart, Redoubt, Parapet* and *Buttress*, clattering down the ramps into some 6 to 7 feet of water some 150 yards off shore. LST *Ravager* moved in toward the Casino Jetty and soon the Centurions were in action on shore. 'B' Squadron in *Salerno* were put down in the fishing harbour and 'A' Squadron in *Ravager* made its way onto the Golf Course. The French LVT made their landings at Port Fouad.

Once ashore the troops were involved in much street fighting with snipers ever present. Air cover continued for all the troops on the ground and progress was being made along the Canal Road. More troops were being brought ashore to Gamil Airfield.

Pressure now was put Britain, France and Israel to cease immediately. Eden was facing criticism not only from his own government, but also from Russia, America and the United Nations.

One letter clearly states that *'The Soviet government considers it necessary to draw your attention to the aggressive war being waged by Britain and France against Egypt...in what position would Britain have found herself if she herself had been attacked by more powerful states possessing every kind of modern destructive weapon? And there are countries now which need to have sent a navy or air force to the coasts of Britain, but could use other means, such as rockets we are fully determined to crush the aggressors and restore peace in the Middle East through use of force. We hope at this critical moment you will display due prudence and draw the corresponding conclusions from this.'*

President Eisenhower wrote *'That to invade Egypt merely because that country had chosen to nationalise a company would be interpreted by the world as power politics and would raise a storm of resentment that, within the Arab states, would result in a long and dreary guerrilla warfare.'*

Another letter sent from Labour Party's Aneurin Bevan states '*...if the Government wants to impose the law of the jungle, they must remember that Britain and France are not the most powerful animals in it. There are much more dangerous creatures prowling around.*'

None of this pressure put on Eden had any effect but it was the United State's ultimatum that brought about the withdrawal. America struck at Britain's fragile economy. It refused to allow the IMF to give emergency loans to Britain unless it called off the invasion. Faced by imminent financial collapse, as the British Treasury saw it, on 5th November 1956 Eden surrendered to American demands and stopped the operation, with his troops stranded half way down the canal.

The French were furious, but obliged to agree; their troops were under British command and the cease-fire was agreed for 2359 hours the following day. The United Nations demanded that British, French, Israeli and Egyptian forces cease hostilities immediately and agreed to a plan to rapidly send peacekeeping forces to Egypt.

	Argyll & Sutherland	RA - 97 Bty
Gordon Highlanders	Highlanders	RA - 34 LAA Regt
	York & Lancaster Regt	RA- 41 Fld. Regt
Cheshire Regt	Royal Warwicks. Regt	RA - 80 LAA
Parachute Regt	1st Bn West Yorks. Regt	Royal Engineers
Guards Independent	Royal Berks Regt	Royal Military
Para	3rd Bn Grenadier	Police
6th Royal Tank Regt	Guards	REME
1st Royal Dragoon	RA - 20 Fld. Regt	Royal Signals
1st Bn Royal West Kent	RA - 23rd Fld. Regt	Royal Corps of
1st Bn Royal Scots	RA - 32 Medium Regt	Signals
1st Bn Royal Fusiliers	RA - 33 Airborne	RAOC
Oxs. & Bucks. L.I.	RA - 33 Para Regt	Royal Pioneer Corps
Highland Light Infantry		RAMC

Meanwhile, more British troops had arrived since the cease-fire bringing the total to approx 13 500, as well as 4 400 vehicles and 10 000 tons of stores. These included units shown in the table above.

General Keightley was instructed to retain an Allied hold on Port Said until UN Forces arrived and prevent any attempts by Egypt to breach the Cease Fire agreement, as well as preparing for the eventual evacuation.

Evacuation finally began on 7th December and by the 14th more than 11 000 had boarded troopships *Dilwara, Ascania* and the carrier *Theseus*, while others flew out by air. Troopships *New Australia*, *Asturias* and *Dunera* followed these. By 22nd December 1956 the last troops had left Port Said and the last ship leaving was the warship HMS *Duchess*. All that now remained in Egypt was the limited number of ships of the Allied Salvage Fleet (operating under the UN Flag) for the purposes of clearing the Canal. They remained there until work was completed on the 21st January 1957.

Upon return to Britain there was no 'Hero's Welcome' for these troops.

And the cost of all this?

The Labour Party estimated bill stood at £328 000 000 (which included Loss of Trade).

Eden was forced to resign as Prime Minister on 9th January 1957, his reputation in tatters. British casualties stood at 16 dead and 96 wounded, while French casualties were 10 dead and 33 wounded. The Israeli losses were 231 dead and 899 wounded. The number of Egyptians killed was 'never reliably established'. Egyptian casualties to the Israeli invasion were estimated at 1 000 - 3 000 dead and 4 000 wounded, while losses to the Anglo-French operation were estimated at 650 dead and 900 wounded 1 000 Egyptian civilians are estimated to have died.

The lighter side of the Crisis

One amusing incident did take place when a pilot supporting the Paras engaged in fierce fighting in a cemetery in Port Said was ordered to stop shooting. Apparently a civilian funeral procession had reached the cemetery in the middle of this battle and there both sides respectfully stopped firing whilst the funeral took place, only to start again once it had left! Only in Egypt!

One of the first aircraft to arrive at Gamil was a *Skyraider* from *Albion*, reacting to a signal from the paratroopers that the local water supply was contaminated and that fresh water was needed urgently. The first thought upon *Albion* was to fit long-range tanks to the *Skyraider*, fill them with water and take them ashore, but although the tanks were new the ship's MO would not pass the water fit for human (or paratrooper) consumption. The ship's Welfare Committee rose to the occasion by offering to send canned beer instead. By packing beer crates in every available space, including up the radar tunnel, and leaving out one observer, they had room for 1 000 cans. At Gamil the Paras were not slow in unpacking the cargo and getting to grips with it. When they were shouting for more beer a deal was struck with the NAAFI at RAF Akrotiri in Cyprus. Four *Skyraiders* went over to collect the beer and on the way back, flying at 8 000 feet a radio message was received from the NAAFI warning that the cans were pressurised and not to fly above 5 000 feet. They chanced it at 6 500 feet, with 5 000 cans between them and never lost a drop - much to the relief of the Paras.

- HMS *Albion* had a memorable visit from General Stockwell in mid-November. Members of the ship's company mounted a special Guard of Honour on the flight deck. They wore their uniforms and caps back to front and marched backwards to 'The Goons' chart success 'I'm Walking Backwards for Christmas'. On being invited to inspect the guard, General Stockwell obliged, entering into the spirit of the occasion by reversing his own cap.
- Over the Christmas period ships of the Fleet were returning to Malta. On a rainy Christmas morning came HMS *Duchess* followed by the carrier HMS *Albion* and the cruiser HMS *Jamaica* with a life size Father Christmas tied to the bow jackstay. On her quarterdeck, the band played Christmas carols. On Boxing Day, HMS *Tyne* still flying the flag of Vice Admiral Dunford-Slater and Forth appeared, sporting a large display of Father Christmas on a sledge hoisted between her funnels.
- As HMS *Crane* steamed away, after being battered by an Israeli Mysteres that mistook her for the Egyptian frigate *Rashid*, it was commented that she '*was a fine sight, with her crumpled stern, her shot holes amidships and aft, her paying off pennant flying, and her ship's company in fine fettle .... I was sorry to lose her.*'
- The Commander of Task Force 324 signalled,

'Blunt in front
Hole behind
Pierced amidships
Never mind.
You start your journey home today.
And hell to Nasser anyway!'

Source: Patricia Jezzard, President of The Canal Zoners
Web site: www.canalzoners.co.uk

Appendix 1

Driving in the Canal Zone

Threats

The Canal Zone was one of the most dangerous places to drive. Traffic Accidents (RTAs) accounted for more deaths and serious injuries, on and off duty than any other factor. This coupled with the added threat of bombs, IEDs, ambush, poor road conditions and summer driving conditions made driving hazardous. RTA procedure required those on board to stop and conduct first aid in a safe location; and contact base stating the location, details of load, any casualties, damage to vehicles and actions being taken at the scene.

Road conditions

Tarmac was poorly maintained; there was little or no street lighting and not many pavements. The roads were riddled with potholes, drainage ditches and humps. Consequently many vehicles overturned and were write-offs.

Dirt tracks were worse and only to be used if operationally essential and had been cleared by Royal Engineer or RAOC explosive ordnance disposal experts.

Road conditions caused by dust and poor visibility meant that drivers had to slow down, keep their distance and close windows.

Safety and driving techniques

All drivers needed to be properly qualified and officers were only allowed to drive in exceptional circumstances. Others who had not received adequate training and vehicle familiarisation prior to deployment were required to make this fact known.

It was necessary to drink plenty of water, wear eye protection and remember that heat would make you feel tired - made worse if helmets were worn.

When driving it was necessary to 'command the road' and stay alert at all times. Drivers needed to remember to select a lower gear on descents and never to drive too close to the edge of the road.

All weapons needed to be loaded and unloaded under supervision prior to entering or exiting a camp. This was due to too many accidental discharges killing or injuring personnel.

Responsibility

Too many servicemen and women were being killed or injured in RTAs. The biggest cause of these accidents was driving too fast for the road conditions. A sensible convoy speed should have been maintained, but this would only happen if they were properly supervised and controlled by officers and NCOs. Too many drivers drove over-aggressively just as Egyptian truck drivers did whose aim was to force our trucks off the road.

Appendix 2

Threats to the British Military

The main threat to our troops was terrorism and espionage.

Terrorism

Counter measures included alert states and personal security measures. Troops were confined to camp and movement restricted. Out of bounds and no-go areas were identified and families either repatriated home or sent to 'safe areas'.

Defenders of Islam issued threat messages such as: 'WARNING -you will have no rest, no sleep. We will get you one by one, slowly but surely. We will hang you by the neck from the Acacia trees. We will finish you off.' Well-organised Egyptian official and unofficial paramilitary groups supplemented the active local terrorists.

Espionage

Attempts were constantly made by seemingly innocent locals to acquire information covertly or illegally in order to assist terrorists. Egyptian labourers supposedly looking for work included terrorists spying on the British.

Collection methods included observation by sharp-eyed watchful informers and other means of surveillance. Nowadays sophisticated means are employed including call phones hidden inside speedometers and even two-way videophones inside a driving mirror!

Photography of installations was another way of gaining insight into what went on inside the wire. Information was also collected by technical intercepts - terrorists listening in to insecure radio traffic.

They gathered open source low-level information by scrutinising newspapers and listening-in to servicemen's conversations in places of entertainment or other public places. Worse still by harvesting official waste rubbish and personal mail.

Improvised explosive devices (IEDs)

IEDs represented a constant threat in the form of roadside bombs, and liquid gas canisters. Grenades were thrown and suicide bombings although rare did occur.

Attacks on troops and Non Governmental Organisations (NGOs)

Kidnapping, torture and mutilation was commonplace. Treatment of HM Forces personnel and civilians was barbaric as evidenced by bodies recovered with hands, arms, feet and breasts severed by knives, saws or axes before they were dumped in the Sweet Water Canal or left by the roadside.

Many innocent family members and civilian workers were stabbed or murdered including a Nun, Sister Anthony, a teacher who was killed while trying to shield children during an attack by grenade throwing thugs armed with rifles.

Counter measures

Apart from road blocks and searches, routine mobile patrols, search-light operations, guard duties and vehicles travelling either in well armed convoys or with a second vehicle following little could be done to maintain safety. The unpredictability of random and frequent ambushes, sniping and kidnapping by individual terrorists or small bands of murderers was relentless.

SD - #0012 - 070726 - C0 - 228/152/9 - PB - 9781910616659 - Matt Lamination